بسم الله الرحمن الرحيم

ربِّ يسِّرْ وأعِنْ يا كريم

ISBN: 978-1492360490

An e-book and Audio book version of
this book is available at www.Hanbalifiqh.com

Table of Contents

"Qaddūmi's Elementary Ḥanbali Primer" 5
The author & his book 5
Format and Sources 6
My service to this book 7
PURITY 10
Water 10
Vessels and Carrion 13
Bathrooms Manners 14
Dental Care 18
Wuḍū' 21
Wiping over the Khuff 29
Invalidators of Wuḍū'' 33
Ghusl 36
Tayammum 43
Removal of Impurity 46
Menses and Postpartum bleeding 49
PRAYER 52
Ruling of Prayer 57
Prayer Times 58
Supererogatory Prayers 59
Conditions of Prayer 63
Pillars of Prayer 64
Obligations of the Prayer 66
Sunan of Prayer 68
Sajda from Forgetfulness 73
Disliked Acts in Prayer 75
Acts that invalidate prayer 77
Congregational Prayer 82
Joining between two prayers 89
Jumu'a Prayer 90
The Two 'Eīd Prayers 96

Time of Prohibition 100
Rulings on the Deceased 101
Prayer over the deceased 103
FASTING 106
Rulings on Fasting 106
Things which invalidate fast 110
ZAKAT 113
Rulings of Zakat 113
Zakat on Livestock 115
Zakat of Grains and Fruit 118
Zakat on Gold, Silver, and Merchandise 120
Zakat al-Fiṭr 121
Zakat Recipients 122
HAJJ 124
Rulings on Those who make Hajj and Umra 124
Pillars of Hajj and Umra 125
Obligations of Hajj and ʿUmra 126
Forbidden Acts while in Ihram 128
Selected Bibliography 132

"Qaddūmi's Elementary Ḥanbali Primer"

The author & his book

Known as "The eminent scholar, the jurist, the polymath, Mūsā ibn ʿĪsā ibn ʿAbdullah Ṣūfān ibn ʿĪsā ibn Salāma ibn ʿŪbayd al-Qaddūmī al-Nābulsī al-Ḥanbalī was born in the village of Kafr Qaddūm in 1265H. Raised in a pious and devout family known for its knowledge and virtue, he learned the rudiments of reading and writing. Later he travelled to Damascus, the primary destination of all Ḥanbalis of that time. He met and studied with numerous scholars, learning from them the disciplines of tawḥīd, tafsīr, ḥadīth, fiqh, inheritance, grammar, and morphology.

Perhaps the more prominent of his teachers were: the famous scholar of inheritance Muḥammad ibn Ḥasan al-Shaṭṭī (d. 1307H), from whom he took fiqh and inheritance; the Muftī of the Levant, Muḥammad ibn Aḥmad al-Manīnī al-Ḥanafī (d. 1316H), from whom he took the studies of tafsīr, ḥadīth, and grammar; the jurist and Musnid of the Levant Salīm ibn Yasīn ibn Ḥāmid al-ʿAṭṭār al-Shafiʿī (d.1307H), from whom he took tafsīr, ḥadīth, and logic, awarding him a general Ijāza as well; as well as the poet, literary figure, and

Musnid ʿAbdulSalām Ibn ʿAbdulRaḥīm al-Shaṭṭī al-Ḥanbali (d.1295H), who awarded him a general, multifaceted Ijāza, known as al-Ijāzat ʿl-Shaṭṭiyya. In addition to these he learned from numerous other scholars.

He later returned to his hometown, and from there settled on Nablus as his home. Joining his cousin Shaykh ʿAbdullah Ṣūfān al-Qaddūmī, he shared the responsibility of teaching in the Jāmiʿ al-Ṣalāḥī. After his cousin migrated to the land of the Ḥijāz, he assumed the position of sole instructor in the Jāmiʿ. His knowledge was sought out by students far and wide. After the Jāmiʿ al-Ṣalāḥī was closed during the first World War, he assumed a private life, continuing to teach in his home until his death in 1336H.

Format and Sources

The original title of this work in Arabic is "*al-ʾAjwibat ʾl-Jaliyya fī ʾl-ʾAḥkām ʾl-Ḥanbaliyya*" or "Clear Answers on Ḥanbali rulings." For convenience I have opted to title it "Qaddūmi's Elementary Ḥanbali Primer" in the English language. This primer is written in the form of questions and answers, and is clearly a product of the author's many years of instruction and Fatwā. Detailing one hundred and six questions on the topics of Ṭahāra, Ṣalāt, Ṣawm, Zakāt, and Ḥajj, the author gave sole importance to clarifying the pillars, obligations, and recommendations in each of these topics. As is the case with most rudimentary texts in Islamic law, the author omitted mention of both textual and rational evidences. This serves a dual purpose: it allows a beginner to grasp the most fundamental issues pertinent to the topic as well as build a foundation for further study.

Al-Qaddūmī summarized much of the material for this primer from the foundational Ḥanbalī text of that period: Dalīl al-Ṭālib of al-ʿAllāma Marʿi Ibn Yusuf al-Karmi al-Ḥanbali (d.1033h). Following that text in most of the pillars, obligations, and recommendations on these topics, this short treatise is a new link in the chain of teaching the Ḥanbalī school. What makes it stand out are the clarifications that the author made to various phrases that, for the beginner, may seem illusive or lengthy. Additionally, he adds a number of tenets and maxims which, along with the explanation of technical and linguistic terms, brings the objectives of the school into the reach of the novice.

My service to this book

In this translation I have relied exclusively on the Dār Aṭlas edition by Nūr al-Dīn Ṭālib, and have compared some of the phrases that were unclear to more advanced texts and their explanations such as Dalīl al-Ṭālib and al-Rawḍ al-Murbiʿ. One point that should be apparent to the reader is that this book is according to one Riwāya of Imām Aḥmad's Madhhab. Learning the legal schools of Islam has a methodology, and that methodology calls for learning the basis of a particular legal school before engaging in high level discussions (both intra-madhhab and comparatively between schools). Engaging in theoretical discussion before building a foundation in the basis of the law is a major pitfall for any student, and can - at times - inculcate pride and pomposity in the student. These character flaws will blind the student from developing the humility and the analytical process necessary for the Faqīh to tackle current issues. High level discussions are reserved for classes with one's teacher after gaining proficiency in the basics.

Keeping this in mind, I've purposely kept explanatory notes at a minimum, although I did clarify some of the terms and issues found in the text if called for. Several issues found in this text are solitary opinions specific to the Ḥanbalī school and are not held by the other canonical legal schools (Ḥanafi, Shafiʿi, and Māliki schools) and as such these issues have explanatory footnotes. The references used are listed in the bibliography at the end of this book.

It is important to note that this book, as well as all books of Islamic law, are not – for the most part - prescriptive. They are descriptive. Fiqh books are used for learning the law. They may at times contains issues that are misunderstood, issues that are derivative and subjective, and issues that are in the face of authentic evidence, wrong. The most important thing that you the reader can do after purchasing this humble text is to sit with a teacher. Someone who will guide you through the text and assist you in the learning process.

He who doesn't thank the people has not thanked Allah. I'd like to thank all those that made this text possible, first and foremost my family who were the first students to review this text with me.

I hope that my service to this book and the Ḥanbali school finds it way into my scale of good deeds on the Day of Judgment. Any mistakes herein are from myself and from Shayṭān. Any good herein is merely the boon of scholars past; God Almighty is its ultimate source, "all good being in His hands."[1]

Joe Bradford

---

[1] - Paraphrased from a ḥadīth found in Muslim from ʿAlī Ibn Abī Ṭālib.

بسم الله الرحمن الرحيم

PURITY

كتاب الطهارة

Water

باب المياه

All praise is due to God alone, may he grace and bless him who after him there is no other prophet:

الحمد لله وحده، والصلاة والسلام على مَنْ لا نبي بعده:

Q1- What is purity, linguistically and technically

س1: ما هي الطَّهارة لغةً وشرعًا؟

A1- Purity, linguistically, is cleanliness.

ج: الطّهارة لغة: النَّظافة.

Technically, it is the removal of ritual impurity and the cessation of actual impurity.

وشرعًا: ارتفاع الحدث، وزوال الخبث.

Ritual impurity is two types:

ثم الحدث قسمان:

1- Greater; that which obligates Ghusl.

2- Lesser; that which obligates Wudū᾽.

1- أكبر: وهو ما أوجب الغسل.

2- وأصغر وهو ما أوجب الوضوء.

Q2- What are the categories of water?

س2: كم أقسام الماء؟ وما هي؟

A2- Water is three categories:

ج: أقسام الماء ثلاثة:

First: Purifying (Ṭahūr)	**الأوَّل:** طهورٌ:
Water which is in its original state is purifying, regardless of whether it poured from the sky or sprang forth from the earth.	وهو الباقي على خلقته الأصلية، سواء نزل من السماء، أو نبع من الأرض.
It is pure in itself, and purifies other than it.	وهو طاهر في نفسه، مطهر لغيره.
It raises ritual impurity and removes actual impurity.	يرفع الحدث، ويزيل الخبث.
Second: Pure (Ṭāhir)	**الثاني:** طاهر: وهو:
1- Water which much of has changed in color, taste, or smell by mixing with a pure substance like Saffron.	1- ما تغيَّر كثير من لونه أو طعمه أو ريحه بمخالطة شيء طاهر كزعفران.
2- Or was scant and was used in raising a ritual impurity.	2- أو كان قليلاً واستُعمل في رفع حدثٍ.
3- Or the entire hand of a legally responsible Muslim is submerged into it after having awoke from a night's sleep before washing it three times with intention and the	3- أو انغمست فيه كل يد المسلم المكلَّف القائم من نوم ليلٍ قبل غسلها ثلاثًا بنية وتسميةٍ، وذلك واجب.

Basmala (which is obligatory)[2].

وهو طاهر في نفسه، غير مطهِّر لغيره.

It is pure in itself, yet does not purify other than it.

يجوز استعمالُه في غير رفع حدثٍ وزوال خبث كطبخ وشربٍ ونحوهما.

It is permissible to use in removing other than ritual impurities and actual impurities, such as cooking, drinking, and the like.

الثالث: نجس.

Third: Impure (Najis)

وهو: ما وقعت فيه نجاسة، وكان قليلاً، وإن لم يتغيّر، أو كثيرًا وتغيَّر أحد أوصافه.

Impure water is that which impurities have fallen into while it was a small amount, even if it does not change. [Water] of large amounts which one of its characteristics have changed [is impure as well].

ولا يرفع الحدث، ولا يزيل الخبث.

It does not remove ritual impurity or actual impurity.

والكثير: ما بلغ قلَّتين فأكثر.

[Water] of large amounts is the volume of two Qulla or

---

2 - Washing the hands three times after a night's sleep is Wājib according to the madhhab. In another Riwāya, it is Mustaḥab. This is based on the ḥadīth of Abū Hurayra in Bukhāri and Muslim.

more of water.

وهما: أحد وسبعون رطلاً وثلاثة أسباع رطل بالنَّابلسي وما وافقه.

[Two Qulla] are seventy one and 3/7th Nabulsi Raṭl[3].

أحكام الآنية وأجزاء الميتة

Vessels and Carrion

س3: ما الذي يباح اتخاذه من الأواني؟

Q3- What sort of vessels are permissible to use.

ج: يباح اتخاذ كل إناء طاهرٍ، واستعماله، إلا آنية الذهب والفضة، فيحرم استعمالهما واتخاذهما.

A3- Every pure vessel is permissible to possess and use except for gold and silver vessels; they are impermissible to use and possess.

س4: ما حكم آنية الكفار وثيابهم؟

Q4- What is the ruling on unbelievers' vessels and clothing?

ج: آنية الكفار وثيابهم طاهرة، ما لم تُعْلَم نجاستها.

A4- Unbelievers' vessels and clothing are pure, as long as their impurity is not known.

---

[3] - This type of Raṭl equals 12 Ūqiyya, one Ūqiyya equaling forty dirham. Two Qulla then is roughly 191.25 liters or around 50 gallons.

س5: ما حكم أجزاء الميتة؟

Q5- What is the ruling on parts of carrion?

ج: عظم الميتة وقرنُهَا نجس.

A5- Bones and horns of carrion are impure.

وكـذا جلـدها، ولا يطهـر بالـدباغ، لكـن لـو دُبِـغَ يبـاح استـعماله فـي اليابسـات دون المائعات.

As well as its skin. It is not purified through tanning. If, however, it was tanned then it is permissible to use with dry-goods (to the exclusion of liquids).

وأما الشعر والصـوف والـريش فطـاهر، إن كـان مـن حيـوان طاهر في الحياة، وإن لم يكـن من مأكولاً كالهرة.

Hair, wool, and feathers are pure if they are from an animal considered pure while alive, even if not edible, like a cat.

أحكام الاستنجاء وآداب التَّخلي

Bathrooms Manners

س6: ما هـو الاسـتنجاء؟ ومـا حكمُهُ؟

Q6- What is Istinjāʾ? What is its ruling?

ج: هـو إزالـة مـا خـرج مـن السبيلين بماء طهورٍ، أو حجر

A6- Istinjāʾ is the removal of urine and excrement with purifying water or permitted rocks or similar

مباح ونحوه كالخرق.	such as cloth.
وهو واجب لكل خارج إن لم يكن ميتًا، أو ريحًا، أو ناشفًا لم يلوث المحلَّ كالحصى.	It is obligatory for everything that is excreted as long as it is not dead, wind, or dry and does not contaminate the area, like stones.
س 7: ما شرط صحتهِ؟	Q7- What is the condition for it to be valid?
ج: شرط صحته الإنقاء:	A7- For it to be valid, it must cleanse
وهو بالماء: عود خشونة المحل كما كان.	using water: the coarseness of the place should return as it was.
وبالحجر: أن يبقى أثرٌ لا يزيله إلا الماء. بشرط:	using rocks: any traces that are left should only be able to be removed by water.
1- أن يمسح ثلاث مسحات تعم كل مسحة المحل.	With the condition: 1- That one wipe three wipes, each wipe covering the place.
2- وأن لا يتجاوز الخارج موضع العادة.	2- That the excrement not surpass the customary area.

والأفضل: أن يستجمر أولاً بالأحجار ثم يُتبعها بالماء.	What is preferred: That one wipes with rocks first[4], then follows with water.
س8: ما هي آداب قاضي الحاجة؟	Q8- What are the requisite manners of a person using the lavatory.
ج: هي:	A8- They are:
1- أن يقدم اليسرى عند دخول الخلاء، ويقول: ((بسم الله، أعوذ بالله من الخبث والخبائث)).	1- Placing the left foot first when entering the bathroom while saying "With God's name, I seek refuge with God from filth and filthy beings."
2- وإذا خرج قدّم اليمنى وقال: ((غفرانك، الحمد لله الذي أذْهَب عني الأذى وعافاني)).	2- When leaving, place the right foot first and say "Your forgiveness! All praise is due to God who removed from me harm and gave me health."
س9: ما يكره لقاضي	Q9- What is disliked for a person relieving himself? What is forbidden?

---

4 - Known as Istijmār, it is the act of cleansing oneself from stool and urine by wiping with a solid object, usually a rock or stone, or something similar like a cloth or paper.

الحاجة؟ وما يحرم عليه؟

ج: يكره له:	A9- It is disliked for him:
1- استقبال الشمس والقمر.	1- To face the sun or the moon.
2- ومهب الريح.	2- To face the direction of the wind.
3- والكلام.	3- To speak.
4- والبول في إناء بلا حاجة.	4- To urinate in a vessel with no need,
5- وفي شقٍّ.	5- in a chasm,
6- ونارٍ.	6- in fire,
7- ورمادٍ.	7- And in coals.
ويحرُم عليه:	It is forbidden for him to
1- استقبال القبلة، واستدبارها في الصحراء بلا حائلٍ.	1- Face the Qibla, or turn his back to it, if in the open without a barrier.
2- وأن يقضي حاجته في طريق مسلوكٍ.	2- To relieve himself in a trodden path.

3- Or in beneficial shade.

3- أو ظل نافع.

4- Or under a fruit bearing tree.

4- وتحت شجرة مثمرةٍ.

5- And to remain in the bathroom longer than necessary.

5- وأن يلبث فوق حاجته.

It is permissible to urinate standing, if safe from being seen or contaminating oneself.

ويجـوز البـول قائمًـا إذا أمِـنَ ناظرًا أو تلويثًا.

Dental Care

أحكام السواك

Q10- What is the ruling on dental hygiene? When is it recommended? What benefit does it have?

س10: مـا حكـم السـواك؟ وفـي أي محـل يتأكـد؟ ومـا فائدته؟

A10- Dental hygiene is recommended at all times, for someone not fasting. If fasting, then it is disliked after midday.

ج: السواك مسنون كل وقتٍ، لغير صائم بعد الزوال فيكره.

It is recommended

ويتأكد:

1- When making Wudū’

1- عند وضوء.

2- وصلاةٍ.	2- Before prayer
3- وقراءة قرآن.	3- Before reciting Quran
4- وانتباه من نوم.	4- When waking
5- وتغير رائحة فم.	5- When the smell of [one's] breath changes.
6- ودخول مسجد.	6- When entering the Masjid
7- ومنزلٍ	7- [When entering one's] home
8- وإطالة سكوتٍ.	8- After prolonged silence
9- وصفرة أسنان.	9- Upon the yellowing of teeth
10- وخلو معدة من طعام.	10- And when the stomach is empty
وفوائده كثيرة، منها:	It has many benefits, from them:
1- أنه يهضم الطَّعام.	1- It assists in digestion
2- ويشد لحمة الأسنان.	2- It tightens the gums
3- وأعظمها: أنه يذكر	3- And the greatest of them: that it reminds

one of the testimony of faith near death.	الشهادة عند الموت.
Q11- What sort of hygiene and grooming are recommended?	س11: ما الذي يسن فعله من التنظيف وتحسين الهيئة؟
It is recommended:	ج: يسنُّ:
1- To shave the abdominal hair.[5]	1- حلق العانة.
2- Plucking the armpits	2- ونتف الإبط.
3- Clipping the fingernails	3- وقص الأظافر.
4- Looking in the mirror	4- والنظر في المرآة.
5- Applying Kohl nightly	5- والاكتحال كلَّ ليلة.
6- Trimming the mustache	6- وحف الشارب.
7- And leaving the beard	7- وإعفاء اللحية.
It is forbidden to shave it, yet there is no harm in taking from anything longer than a fist length.	وحرم حلقُها، ولا بأس بأخذ ما زاد على القبضة منها.

[5] - Including the hair from the navel to that surrounding the anus.

أحكام الوضوء	***Wuḍū***ʾ
س 12: كم فرائض الوضـوء؟ وما هي:	Q12- How many obligations of Wuḍūʾ are there? What are they?
ج: فـروض الوضـوء سـتة، وهي:	A12- Obligations of Wuḍūʾ are six:
1- غسـل الوجـه، ومنـه: المضمضة والاستنشاق.	1- Washing the face, including rinsing the mouth and the inside of the nose[6].
2- وغسـل اليـدين مـع المرفقين، والمرفق: هو العظم الفاصل بين الدراع والعضد.	2- Washing the hands along with the elbows. The elbow: the joint separating the forearm from the bicep.
3- ومسح جميع ظاهر الرأس،	3- Wiping over the entire head, including the ears

[6] - Rinsing the mouth (Maḍmaḍa) and the inside of the nose (Istinshāq) are obligatory acts (Furūḍ) in both Wuḍūʾ and Ghusl, due to the ḥadīth in Abū Dāwūd "When you make Wuḍūʾ then make Maḍmaḍa" and in Muslim "When you make Wuḍūʾ then rinse your nose." A command entails obligation, and these ḥadīth along with the command in al-Māida "Wash your faces" entails that rinsing the mouth and nose are obligatory, as they are part of the face.

ومنه الأذنـان: والبيـاض الـذي فوقهما.	and the bare skin above them[7].
4- وغســـل الـــرجلين مـــع الكعبـــين، وهمـــا: العظمـــان الناتئان في أسفل الساق.	4- Washing the feet to the ankles; the two protruding bones at the end of the shins.
5- والترتيب بين الأعضاء.	5- Washing the limbs in order.
6- والمولاة، وهي: أن لا يؤخر غسل عضوٍ إلـى أن يجـف مـا قبله بزمن معتدلٍ.	6- And continuity: i.e. to not delay the washing of one limb until the limb before it dries in a moderate amount of time[8].
س13: مـا الـذي يجـب فـي	Q13- What things are required in Wuḍū᾿?

---

[7] - This is particular to the Madhhab, due to the ḥadīth in Abū Dāwūd "The ears are from the head"

[8] - Breaking continuity in Wuḍū᾿ invalidates the Wuḍū᾿, even if done forgetfully. Other schools differentiate between breaking continuity intentionally and doing so forgetfully. Continuity (Muwālā) is defined as to not delay the washing of a limb until the limb before it has dried. Such delay would be from searching for water, removing impurities or dirtiness, i.e. something not part and parcel of the act of Wuḍū᾿, not the type of delay from performing a sunna such as combing through the beard with water.

الوضوء؟

ج: يجب فيه التسمية فقط.

A13- Saying the Basmalah is the only requirement.[9]

وتسقط بتركها سهواً، أو جهلاً لا عمداً.

It becomes non-requisite when forgotten unintentionally or out of ignorance, not when left off purposely.

س14: كم شروط الوضوء؟

Q14- What and how many conditions are there for Wuḍū'?

ج: شروطه ثمانية، وهي:

A14- There are eight conditions, they are:

1- انقطاع ما يوجبه من بول وريح وحيض ونفاس ونحو ذلك.

1- Cessation of what necessitates it whether urine, wind, menses, post partum bleeding, or similar.

2- والنية.

2- Intention

3- والإسلام.

3- Islam

4- والعقل.

4- Sound mind

---

[9] - The Basmala, i.e. saying "Bismillah," before commencing Wuḍū' is Wājib, due the ḥadīth in Abū Dawūd.

5- والتمييز، أي: بلوغ سبع سنين.	5- Discernment; i.e. reaching seven years.
6- والماء الطهور المباح.	6- Purifying, permissible[10] water.
7- وإزالة ما يمنع وصول الماء من شمع أو عجين أو نحوهما.	7- Removing anything that prevents the water from reaching such as wax, dough, or similar.
8- والاستنجاء أو الاستجمار.	8- [As well as] Istinjāʾ and Istijmār.
س15: كم سنن الوضوء؟ وما هي؟	Q15- What are and how many recommended acts are there in Wuḍūʾ?
ج: سننه ثمانية عشر، وهي:	A15- Recommended acts are eighteen, they are:
1- استقبال القبلة.	1. Facing the Qibla
2- والسواك.	2. Using Siwāk

[10] - Using permissible water, i.e. water not stolen, usurped, or misappropriated, is a condition for Wuḍūʾ according to the Madhhab. The same rule applies to Tayammum, Istinjāʾ and Istijmār as well.

3- وغسل الكفين ثلاثًا، لغير قائم من نوم ليل، فيجب بنية وتسمية – كما تقدم-.	3. Washing the hands 3 times; for someone waking from a night's sleep, this is obligatory with the requisite intention and saying the Basmala, as mentioned earlier.
4- والبداءة بالمضمضة والاستنشاق قبل غسل الوجه.	4. Starting with rinsing the mouth and nose before washing the face.
5- والمبالغة فيهما لغير الصائم.	5. Exaggerating rinsing [the mouth and nose] for someone not fasting
6- والمبالغة في سائر الأعضاء.	6. Exaggerating the washing of all other limbs
7- والزيادة في ماء الوجه.	7. Using more water for the face
8- وتخليل اللحية الكثيفة.	8. Passing water through a thick beard
9- وتخليل أصابع اليدين والرجلين.	9. Passing water through the fingers and toes.
10- وأخذ ماءٍ جديدٍ للأذنين.	10. Taking new water for the ears.

11- وتقـديم اليمنـى علـى اليسرى من اليدين والرجلين.	11. Washing the right hand and right foot before the left.
12- ومجاوزة محـل الفـرض في الأعضاء الأربعة.	12. Washing beyond the obligatory boundaries of the four limbs.
13- والغسلة الثانية والثالثة.	13. A second and third washing
14- واستصـحاب النيـة إلـى آخر الوضوء.	14. Maintaining intention until Wuḍū᾿ is finished
15- والإتيان بالنية عند غسـل الكفين.	15. Making intention when washing the hands.
16- والنطق بها سرًا.	16. Pronouncing it secretly/to oneself
17- وقول ما ورد بعد فراغه:	17. Saying the transmitted after finishing:
وهو: ((أشـهد أن لا إلـه إلا اللّٰه وحده لا شريك له، وأشـهد أن محمدًا عبـده ورسـوله، اللهـم	Namely "I testify that there is none worthy of worship but God alone, and I testify that Muhammad is his slave and messenger. O God make me from the repentant, and make me from your purified

اجعلني من التوابين، واجعلني من عبادك المتطهرين)) مع رفع بصره إلى السماء.	servants." Raising his gaze to the heavens. [11]
18- وأن يتولى وضوءه بنفسه.	18. And to make wuḍū' by oneself
س16: أخبرني عن صفة الوضوء الكامل؟	Q16- Tell me how to make a complete wuḍū'.
ج: صفته:	Its description is as follows:
1- أن ينوي الوضوء للصلاة.	1. [One should] make intention for prayer
2- ثم يقول: بسم الله.	2. then say: Bismillah
3- ويغسل كفيه ثلاثًا.	3. then wash the hands thrice
4- ثم يتمضمض، ويستنشق ثلاثًا ثلاثًا.	4. Then rinse the mouth and nose three times each.

[11] - Narrated by Muslim, Abu Dawūd, and al-Tirmidhi from Umar ibn al-Khaṭṭāb.

5- ثم يغسل وجهه ثلاثًا من منبت شعر الرأس المعتاد إلى منتهى الذَّقن طولاً، ومن الأذن إلى الأذن عرضًا.

5. Then wash the face three times from the customary hairline to the chin lengthwise, and from ear to ear across.

6- ثم يغسل يديه مع مرفقيه ثلاثًا.

6. Then wash the hands along with the elbows thrice

7- ثم يمسح جميع ظاهر رأسه، يمر يديه من مقدَّمه إلى قفاه، ويعيدهما.

7. Then wipe the entirety of the head, passing the hands over the front to the back, then back again.

8- ويدخل سبابتيه في صماخ أذنيه، ويمسح بإبهاميه ظاهرهما.

8. [One should] insert the index finger in the crevasses of his ear, and uses the thumb to wipe the back of the ear.

9- ثم يغسل رجليه مع كعبيه ثلاثًا.

9. And then wash the feet including the ankles thrice.

Wiping over the Khuff

أحكام المسح على الخفين

Q17- What is the ruling of wiping over the Khuff[12]?

س17: ما حكم المسح على الخفين؟

A17- It is permissible with seven conditions:

ج: يجوز بشروط سبعة، وهي:

1. Wearing them after complete purity made with water.

1- لبسهما بعد كمال الطهارة بالماء.

2. That they cover the obligatory limb

2- وسترهما لمحل الفرض.

3. The ability to walk in them customarily

3- وإمكان المشي بهما عرفًا.

4. That they stay on by themselves

4- وثبوتهما بنفسهما.

5. That they are permissible[13]

5- وإباحتهما.

---

[12] - A Khuff is a sock made of leather that covers up to and including the ankle.

[13] - Refer to previous footnotes on this concept. Wiping over impermissible footwear is invalid.

6- وطهارة عينهما.	6. That the material they are made of be pure
7- وعدم وصفهما البشرة.	7. That they do not allow the skin to show
س18: كم مدّة المسح عليهما؟ وما المقدار الذي يجب مسحه؟	Q18- How long is wiping over valid for? How much must be wiped over?
ج: يمسح مقيم وعاص بسفره يومًا وليلة من حين حدث بعد لبس.	A18- A resident, as well as a person traveling for sinful reasons, may wipe for one day and night from the time of impurity after wearing.
ويمسح مسافر سفر قصر، ثلاثة أيام بلياليها، ومسافة القصر: يومان معتدلان بسير الأثقال ودبيب الأقدام.	A traveler, on a trip in which he may shorten, wipes for three days and nights. The distance which permits shortening prayers is two median days in which heavy loads are carried and feet carry the traveler.
ويجب مسح أكثر أعلاه، ولا يجزئ مسح أسفله ولا عقبه،	When wiping, it is mandatory to wipe most of the top[14]. Wiping the bottom or the heel is not valid, nor

14 - The Madhhab is that most of the Khuff must be wiped, while others approximate the area to be wiped differently: All, three fingers, or the least to be linguistically acceptable.

ولا يسن ذلك.	is it encouraged.
س19: مـا يُبطـل المسـح عليهما؟	Q19- What invalidates wiping over them?
1- ما أوجب الغسل.	1- Something that obligates Ghusl.
2- أو ظهـور بعـض محـل الفرض.	2- Or part of the obligatory area being exposed.
3- أو انقضاء مدة المسح.	3- Or the period of wiping expiring.
س20: هل يجوز المسح على غير الخفين؟	Q20- Is it permissible to wipe over other than the Khuff?
ج: نعم، يجـوز المسـح على الجبيـرة، وهـي: أخشـاب أو	A20- Yes, it is permissible to wipe over the dressing, [which is] a board or a bandage fixed to a break or a cut[15].

[15] - This is based on the madhhab allowing the Jawrab and the Khimār to be wiped over. The Khimār is a woman's head covering, what many would call Ḥijāb; wiping over it is expressly permitted in Saḥīḥ Muslim. The Jawrab is footwear like the Khuff, but not made of leather. Wiping over the Jawrab is narrated from nine of the companions of the Prophet ﷺ, and is supported by the ḥadīth narrated by Aḥmad that the Prophet wiped over the Jawrab and the sandal.

خرق تربط على الكسر أو الجرح.

س21: أخبرني عن حكم المسح عليها؟

Q21: Tell me the ruling for wiping over them?

ج: إن وضعها على طهارة، ولم تتجاوز محل الحاجة، غسل الصحيح، ومسح على الجريح.

A21: If [the bandage, etc] was placed while in a state of purity, and does not extend farther than needed, then one washes the healthy portion and wipes over the rest.

وإن تجاوزت وخيف الضرر بنزعها، وجب مع المسح التيمم للزائد.

If it covers more than needed, and it is feared that if removed some harm would result, it is obligatory to make Tayammum along with wiping over the extra.

وإن وضعها على غير طهارة غسل الصحيح، وتيمم بلا مسح تجاوزت أم لا.

If placed while not in purity then one washes the healthy portion and makes Tayammum without wiping [over the bandage, etc] at all, regardless of the extent that it reaches to.

باب نواقض الوضوء

Invalidators of Wudū'

س22: كم نواقض الوضوء؟

Q22: How many things invalidate the Wudū'?

ج: نـواقض الوضـوء ثمانيـة، وهي:

A22: Invalidators of Wudū' are eight:

1- الخارج من السـبيلين قلـيلاً كــان أو كثيــرًا، طــاهرًا أو نجسًا.

1- That excreted from the two orifices, regardless of whether sparse or profuse, whether najis or pure[16].

2- وخروج النجاسة مـن بقيـة البدن، فإن كـان الخـارج بـولاً أو غـائطًـا نقــض مطلقًــا وإن كان غيرهمـا كالـدَّم والقـيء، نقض إن كثـر عنـد كـل أحـدٍ بحسب نفسه.

2- Impurity excreted from the rest of the body. If it is urine or stool, it invalidates Wudū' in total. If other than those two – such as blood, pus, etc.- then if profuse it invalidates and if not then no; each to its own extent[17].

---

16 - This includes all substances that come out of the urethra or anus, including but not limited to urine, defecate, pre-ejaculation, ejaculation, and stones.

17 - Due to two ḥadīth in al-Tirmidhi: the first, Thawbān said that the Prophet vomited, then made Wuḍū', the second, his ﷺ statement to Faṭima "This is a vein. Make Wuḍū' for every prayer."

3- وزوال العقل بجنون، أو تغطيته بنحو نوم، ما لم يكن يسيرًا عرفًا من جالس متمكن أو قائم.	3- Loss of consciousness through insound mind, or shrouding [consciousness] as is the case with sleep, as long as it is not slight sleep conventionally acceptable while sitting firmly or standing.
4- ومس فرج الآدمي قبُلاً أو دبُرًا باليد بلا حائل.	4- Touching the private parts of a human being front or back with the bare unprotected hand[18].
5- ولمس الذَّكر بشرة الأنثى، والأنثى بشرة الذكر بشهوة، ولو كان الملموس ميتًا أو عجوزًا أو محرمًا.	5- A male touching the skin of a female, and the female a male's skin; with desire, even if deceased, old or a Maḥram[19].
6- وغسل الميت أو بعضه.	6- Washing the dead or a portion thereof[20].

---

[18] - Due to the ḥadīth of Busra in al-Tirmidhi "Whoever touches their private parts must make Wuḍū'" Excluded from this are children, due to the difficulty of caring for diaper changing and the like.

[19] - A Maḥram is one who you are forbidden to marry, whether male or female.

[20] - Regardless of whether the deceased is old or young, male or female, Muslim or not. The probability of inadvertently touching the ʿAwra while doing so is high, so it was judged to break the Wuḍū' similar to sleep

7- وأكل لحم الإبل ولو نيئًا.	7- Eating camel's meat even if raw[21].
8- والردة عن الإسلام والعياذ بالله تعالى.	8- And apostasy from Islam (refuge is sought with God the Most High)[22].
وكل ما أوجب الغسل أوجب الوضوء إلا الموت.	Everything that necessitates Ghusl, necessitates Wuḍū᾿, except for death.
س23: ما حكم مَنْ شك في الطَّهارة؟	Q23: What is the ruling on the person who doubts his purity?
ج: مَنْ تيَّقن الطهارة وشكّ في الحدث، أو تيقّن الحدث وشكّ في الطهارة، عمل بما تيقن.	A23: Whoever is certain of his purity and doubts ritual impurity or is certain of ritual impurity and doubts his purity, acts according to his certainty.
س24: ما يحرم على المحدث فعله؟	Q24: What is forbidden for a person in ritual impurity to do?

causing minor ritual impurity (al-ḥadath al-aṣghar). No dissent is known amongst the Ṣaḥaba on this issue.

21 - Imam Ahmad said "There are two authentic ḥadīth narrated on this, that of al-Barā᾿ and the ḥadīth of Jābir." The former is found in the Musnad of Aḥmad, while the latter in Ṣaḥīḥ Muslim

22 - Purity is an act, and apostasy invalidates all acts.

ج: يحـــرم علـــى المحـــدث حدثًا أصغر أو أكبر:	A24: It is forbidden for the person in ritual impurity, major or minor, to do any of the following:
1- الصلاة.	1- Ritual prayer
2- والطواف.	2- Tawāf
3- ومـــس المصـــحف بـــلا حائل.	3- And touching the Musḥaf barehanded.
وعلى المحدث حدثًا أكبر:	Anyone with major ritual impurity [is forbidden from]:
1- قراءة القرآن.	1- Reading the Quran
2- والجلوس في المسجد بلا وضوءٍ.	2- And sitting in the Masjid without Wuḍū'.

باب الغسل — *Ghusl*

س25: كم موجبات الغســل؟ وما هي؟	Q25- How many things necessitate Ghusl? What are they?
ج: موجبـــات الغســـل ســـبعة،	A25- Those things which necessitate Ghusl are:

وهي:

1- انتقال المني من مقرّه.

1- The shifting of semen from [the testicles to other than them][23].

2- وخروجه من مخرجه المعتاد بلذة، فإن خرج لغير ذلك لم يوجب الغُسْل.

2- [Semen] exiting its natural outlet accompanied by pleasure. If [semen is excreted] without [pleasure] then Ghusl is not necessary[24].

3- وتغييب الحشفة، أو قدرها من مقطوعها بلا حائل، في فرج أصلي ولو دبرًا، أو لميتٍ، أو بهيمةٍ، أو طائر!

3- Insertion of the glans, or its equivalent length if amputated, without a barrier, in a natural genitalia, even if a rectum, or dead or animal or bird.

4- وإسلام الكافر، ولو مرتدًا.

4- Accepting Islam by an Unbeliever, even if an apostate.

---

23 - This is related from Ḥarb al-Kirmāni from Imam Aḥmed. Shaykh Taqi al-dīn Ibn Taymiyya held that Ḥayḍ was similar. Al-Muwaffaq Ibn Qudāma held that Ghusl does not become obligatory unless semen is ejaculated and exits the urethra.

24 - Meaning if orgasm is reached, semen transfers from the testicles to the urethra, Ghusl is made, then after Ghusl semen drips out, another Ghusl is not necessary, as it was not excreted with pleasure.

5- والحيض.	5- Menses
6- والنفاس.	6- Post partum bleeding
7- والموت، تعبُّدًا.	7- And death, ritually.
س26: كم شروط الغسل؟ وما هي؟	Q26- How many conditions of Ghusl are there? What are they?
ج: شروط الغسل سبعة، وهي:	A26- Conditions for Ghusl are seven. They are:
1- انقطاع ما يوجبه.	1- Cessation of what obliges it.
2- والنية.	2- Intention[25]
3- والإسلام.	3- Islam
4- والعقل.	4- Sound mind
5- والتمييز.	5- Discernment

[25] - I.e. intention to remove both major and minor ritual impurity. If the intention made is to remove only major ritual impurity, Wuḍū' must be made for the minor ritual impurity.

6- والماء الطهور المباح.

6- [Use of] Purifying, permissible water

7- وإزالة ما يمنع وصول الماء إلى الجسد.

7- And removal of anything preventing water from reaching the body[26].

س27: ما الذي يجب في الغُسْل؟

Q27- What is obligatory when making Ghusl?

ج: يجب فيه شيء واحد، وهو التسمية.

A27- There is one thing which is obligatory, namely saying "Bismillah."

وتسقط سهواً وجهلاً، لا عمداً.

Its obligation does not apply when forgotten or not performed due to [the person's] ignorance, not when left off intentionally.

س28: ما فرض الغسل؟

Q28- What is the Farḍ of Ghusl?

ج: فرضه شيء واحد، وهو: أن يعمّ [بالماء] جميع بدنه، وداخل فمه وأنفه.

Farḍ is one thing: that water encompasses the entire body, including the inside of the mouth and nose.

---

26 - Including wax or polish on the skin or nails.

س29: كم سُنَنُ الغسل؟ وما هي؟	How many Sunan of Ghusl are there and what are they?
ج: سننه سبعة، وهي:	Sunan of Ghusl are seven:
1- الوضوء قبله.	1- Making Wuḍū᾿ beforehand
2- وإزالة ما على الفرج والبدن من منِّي ونجاسة.	2- Removal of anything on the genitalia and body from semen or impurities.
3- وإفراغ الماء على رأسه ثلاثًا، وعلى بقية بدنه ثلاثًا.	3- Pouring water over the head three times, and over the rest of the body three times.
4- والتيامن.	4- Starting with the right
5- والموالاة.	5- Order
6- وإمرار اليد على الجسد.	6- Rubbing the hand over the body
7- وإعادة غسل رجليه بمكان آخر.	7- And washing the feet again in another location
س30: كم الأغسال	Q30- How many recommended Ghusl are there? What are they?

المسنونات؟ وما هي؟

ج: الأغسال المسنونات ستة عشر، وهي:

A30- There are sixteen recommended Ghusl:

1- الغُسْلُ لصلاة جمعة في يومها، لذكرٍ حضرها.

1- Ghusl for Jumu'a prayer on the same day, for a male that will attend.

2- والغُسل لأجل غسل ميتٍ.

2- Due to washing a corpse.

3- ولصلاة عيد في يومه.

3- For praying ʿEīd on the same day.

4- ولصلاة كسوفٍ.

4- For praying Kusūf

5- واستسقاء.

5- [For praying] Istisqāʾ

6- ولجنونٍ.

6- [Due to] insound mind

7- وإغماء.

7- [Due to] loss of consciousness

8- والاستحاضة لكل صلاة.

8- [Due to] Istiḥāḍa[27] for every prayer.

---

27 - Istiḥāḍa is a general term for menstrual disorders with extremely long, sporadic, or painful periods encompassing Polymenorrhea, Hypermenorrhea, Dysmenorrhea, and Metrorrhagia.

9- والإحرامِ.	9- for Ihram
10- ولدخول مكة – ولو مع حيض.	10- For entering Makka, even if menstruating.
11- ولدخول حرمها.	11- For entering its Haram.
12- ولوقوفٍ بعرفة.	12- For standing at ʿArafa.
13- ولطواف زيارةٍ.	13- For making Tawāf al-Ziyāra.
14- ولطواف وداعٍ.	14- For Tawāf al-Widāʿ.
15- ولمبيتٍ بمزدلفة.	15- For staying at Muzdalifa.
16- ولرمي جمارٍ.	16- And for throwing the Jamarāt.
ويتيمم للكل استحبابًا للحاجة.	Tayammum is recommended and can be made for each [of the previous] when needed.

باب التيمم

Tayammum[28]

س31: كم شروط صحة التيمم؟ وما هي؟

Q31- How many conditions for the validity of Tayammum are there? What are they?

ج: شروط صحة التيمم ثمانية، وهي:

A31- The conditions for the validity of Tayammum are eight. They are:

1- النية.

1- Intention

2- والإسلام.

2- Islam

3- والعقل.

3- Sound mind

4- والتمييز.

4- Discernment

5- والاستنجاء أو الاستجمار.

5- Istinjāʾ and Isitjmaar

6- دخول وقت الصلاة المتيمم لها.

6- Entrance of the time of prayer for which Tayammum is being made.

7- وعدم القدرة على استعمال

7- Inability to use water.

---

28 - Tayammum linguistically means to pursue or seek out. Legally it is defined as: Wiping the face and hands with dust in a specified manner.

الماء.	
8- وأن يكون:	8- And that Tayammum be made with:
أ) بتراب.	a) Dirt
ب) مباحٍ.	b) Which is permissible
ج) غير مُسْتَعْمَلٍ.	c) Unused
د) ولا محترقٍ.	d) Not burned
هـ) له غبار يعلق باليد.	e) Having dust which adheres to the hand.
س32: ما واجب التيمم؟	Q32- What are the obligations of Tayammum?
ج: يجب فيه التسمية.	A32- Saying Bismillah
وتسقط سهوًا وجهلاً، لا عمدًا.	It becomes non-requisite when forgotten unintentionally or due to ignorance, not when left off purposely.
س33: كم فروض التيمم؟ وما هي؟.	Q33- How many Furūḍ of Tayammum are there? What are they?

ج: فروضه خمسة، وهي:	They are five:
1- مسح الوجه دون الفم.	1- Wiping the face, not including the mouth.
2- ومسح اليدين إلى الكوعين.	2- Wiping the hands including the wrists[29].
3- والترتيب.	3- Sequence
4- والموالاة في الطهارة الصغرى.	4- Order during the lesser purification.
5- وتعيين النية لما يتيمَّم له، من حدث أصغر، أو أكبر، أو من نجاسة على البدن.	5- Specifying the intention for that which Tayammum is being made for, either minor or major ritual impurity, or from an impurity on the body.
س34: كم مبطلات التيمم؟ وما هي؟	Q34- How many things invalidate Tayammum, and what are they?
ج: مبطلاته خمسة، وهي:	A34- Invalidators [of Tayammum] are five. They

---

[29] - Wiping the face and hands is done after striking the open palms on dust or soil once, due to the ḥadīth of ʿAmmār in Bukhari and Muslim.

are:

1- ما أبطل الوضوء.	1- Whatever invalidates Wuḍū'.
2- ووجود الماء.	2- The presence of water.
3- وخروج الوقت.	3- Expiry of the [allotted] time.
4- وزوال العذر المبيح.	4- Cessation of the dispensation allowing it.
5- وخلع نحو الخف إن تيمّم وهو لابسه.	5- And removing the like of a Khuff, if a person made Tayammum while wearing one[30].

فصل في إزالة النّجاسة — *Removal of Impurity*

س35: كيف يطهُر المتنجس؟

Q35 - How are impurities purified?

ج: إذا كانت النجاسة من الكلب والخنزير وما تولّد منهما أو من أحدهما يُغسل

A35 - If the impurity is from a dog or a pig, or one of its offspring, the impurity is washed seven times, once with pure soil.

---

[30] - Tayammum, although performed on two limbs (i.e. the hands and the face) applies equally to rest of them, as it is a substitute for Wuḍū'.

المتنجس سبع مراتٍ إحداهن بترابٍ طهور.

وإن كانت من غير ذلك، يغسل سبعًا بالماء فقط.

If from other than them, then it is washed seven times with water only.

ويكفي في بول صبي لم يأكل الطعام نضحه وغمره بالماء.

For the urine of an infant boy who is not weaned, it is sufficient to sprinkle and dampen with water.

وتطهُر أرض ونحوها بإزالة عين النجاسة بالماء.

The ground and similar are purified by removing an impure substance with water.

س36: ما الطاهر وما النجس من الحيوان؟

Q36 - What animals are pure and which are impure?

ج: ما لا يؤكل لحمُه من الطير والبهائم مما فوق الهرة نجس.

A36 - Animals whose meat is not eaten, whether avian or cattle, being larger than a cat, are impure.

وما دونها كالفأرة طاهر.

Anything smaller than [a cat] – such as a mouse - is pure.

وكل ميتةٍ نجسة إلا:

Every carrion is impure except:

1- ميتة الآدمي.	1. The corpse of a human
2- والسمك.	2. Fish
3- والجرادُ.	3. Locusts
4- وما لا دم له سائل، كالعقرب.	4. And creatures without flowing blood, like scorpions

س37: ما حكم الخارج مما يؤكل لحمه؟

Q37 - What of the excrements of animals which are eaten?

ج: ما أكل لحمه: فبوله وروثه، وكل خارج منه طاهر، إلا الدم والقيح، لكن يعفى عن يسيره في الصلاة.

A37 - Animals whose meat is consumed: their urine, dung, and excrements are pure except for blood and pus; minute amounts are pardoned for prayer.

س38: ما حكم الخارج مما لا يؤكل لحمه؟

Q38- What of excrements of animals whose meat is not consumed?

ج: كل خارجٍ منه نجس، إلا مني الآدمي ولبنُه فطاهر.

A38- Every excrement from them is impure, except the human ejaculate and human milk, for they are pure.

The presence of minute amounts of blood and pus are pardoned during prayer, if they originated from something pure while alive.

ويعفى في الصلاة عن يسير الدّم والقيح منه، إن كان طاهرًا في الحياة.

Menses and Postpartum bleeding

باب الحيض والنفاس

Q39- What is Menses?

س39: ما هو الحيض؟

A39- Naturally occurring blood exiting a healthy woman at specific times, not from childbirth.

ج: هــو دم طبيعــة وجبلــة، يخرج مـن المـرأة مـع الصـحة من غير سبب ولادة في أوقاتٍ معلومة.

There is no menses before nine years of age.

ولا حيض قبل تسع.

Nor after fifty[31]

ولا بعد خمسين سنة.

Nor during pregnancy.

ولا مع حملٍ.

Q40- What is the minimum period of menses and what is the maximum, and what

س40: كمـــا أقـــلُّ مـــدة

---

[31] - Thus any bleeding seen thereafter is considered Istiḥāḍa.

الحـيض؟ ومـا أكثرهـا؟ ومـا غالبُها؟

is the norm?

ج: أقلُّها يوم وليلة.

A40- The minimum is one day and night,

وأكثرها خمسة عشر يومًا.

the maximum is 15 days,

وغالبُها ستٌّ أو سبع.

and the norm is 6-7 days.

س41: كـم أقـلُّ الطهـر بـين الحيضتين؟

Q41- What is the minimum period of purity between two menstrual cycles?

ج: أقله ثلاثة عشر يومًا.

A41 - The minimum is thirteen days,

وغالبُه بقية الشَّهر.

the norm is the rest of the month,

ولا حدَّ لأكثره.

and there is no limit to its maximum.

س42: مـا هـو النِّفـاس؟ ومـا أكثره؟ وما أقلُّه؟

Q42- What is post partum bleeding? What is its minimum and maximum?

ج: هو دم يخرج مع الولادة أو قبلها بيومين أو ثلاثةٍ.

A42- Blood which exits after childbirth or before it by two or three days.

وأكثره أربعون يومًا.	Its maximum is 40 days,
ولا حد لأقلّه.	and there is no minimum.
س43: ما يحرم بالحيض والنفاس؟	Q43- What is forbidden while menstruating or during post partum bleeding?
ج: يحرم أشياء، منها:	A43- Certain things are prohibited, namely:
1- الوطء.	1. Intercourse[32]
2- والصلاة.	2. Ritual prayer
3- والصوم.	3. Fasting
4- والطواف.	4. Tawaf
5- وقراءة القرآن.	5. Reading the Quran
6- ومس المصحف.	6. Touching the Musḥaf
7- والجلوس في المسجد.	7. And sitting in the masjid

---

32 - Not included in this is foreplay. It is permissible to enjoy fondling and foreplay everywhere except for the private parts, due to the ḥadīth in Muslim "Do everything but intercourse."

ومتى طهرت يجب عليها قضاء الصوم لا الصلاة.

Whenever she becomes clean, then she must make up fasting, not prayer.

كتاب الصلاة

PRAYER

س44: ما حكم الأذان والإقامة؟

Q44- What is the ruling on Adhān and Iqāma?

ج: حكم الأذان والإقامة أنهما فرضا كفاية في الحضَر على الرِّجال الأحرار.

A44- The ruling for the Adhān and the Iqāma is that they are Farḍ Kifāya[33] during residency for free males.

ويسنان للمنفرد، وفي السَّفر.

They are Sunnah for those praying by themselves, and when traveling[34].

ويكرهان للنساء، ولو بلا رفع صوت.

They are disliked for women, even if they do not raise their voice.

---

[33] - al-Ṭūfī defines Farḍ Kifāya as: Acts the Sharīʿa aims to implement due to the benefit they contain. Individuals are not singularly accountable for performing them, like Janāza prayer and Jihād, not Jumuʿa or Ḥajj.

[34] - Because they were legislated for announcing the beginning of prayer time to a group, while alone or when traveling these two reasons are not applicable.

ولا يصحان إلا:	They are not valid unless:
1- مرتبين.	1- They are performed in sequence.
2- متواليين عرفًا.	2- In order, as is customary.
3- وأن يكونا من واحد، بنيةٍ منه.	3- And that they are made by one person, who has the requisite intention to perform them.
أي: لو أذّن واحد بعض الأذان أو الإقامة، وأتمهما آخر لم يصحا.	That is: If one person gives part of the Adhān or the Iqāma, and another finished it, then they are not valid.
س45: ما يشترط في المؤذّن؟	Q45- What conditions apply to the Mu'adhin?
ج: يشترط في المؤذن ستة شروطٍ:	A45- The following six conditions apply to the Mu'adhin:
1- كونه مسلمًا.	1- Being a Muslim
2- ذكرًا.	2- Male

3- عاقلاً.	3- Of sound mind
4- مميزًا.	4- Of an age of discerment
5- ناطقًا.	5- Speaking
6- عدلاً ولو ظاهرًا.	6- And upright, even if only apparently[35]

س46: هـل يصـح الأذان والإقامة قبل الوقت أم لا؟

Q46- Are the Adhān and Iqāma valid if given before their time?

ج: لا يصحان قبـل الوقـت، إلا أذان الفجر، فيصح بعد نصـف الليل.

A46- They are not valid if performed before their time, except for the Adhān of Fajr, which is acceptable after the middle of the night.

س47: ما ركن الأذان؟

Q47 - What is the pillar of the Adhān?

ج: ركنه: رفع الصوت بـه، مـا لم يؤذّن لحاضرٍ.

A47 - Its pillar: raising the voice while performing it, if not performing it for someone in his presence.

ويسنُّ كون المؤذّن:

It is preferred that the

---

[35] - An openly sinful person's Adhān is not valid, just as his testimony is invalid.

Muʾadhin be:

1- صيّتا.

1- Of strong voice

2- أمينًا.

2- Trustworthy

3- عالمًا بالوقت.

3- Knowledgeable of the time.

4- متطهرًا.

4- In a state of purity

5- قائمًا فيهما.

5- And standing while performing them.

س48: ما يُسَنّ لمن سمع المؤذّن أو المقيم؟

Q48- What is recommended for the one who hears the Adhān or the Iqāma?

ج: يسنّ للمؤذّن، ولمن سمعه، أو سمع المقيم أن يقول مثله.

A48- It is recommended for the Muʾadhin and the one who hears him (or the one making the Iqāma and the one how hears him) to say the like of what he is saying

إلا في الحيعلة، فيقول: لا حول ولا قوة إلا بالله.

Except during "Come to prayer/success" he should say: "There is no movement or strength except by Allah"

وإلا في التثويب، وهو قول المؤذّن في أذان الفجر: الصلاة

And when the Muadhin says during the Adhān of Fajr "Prayer is better than sleep" he says "You've spoken

خير من النّوم، فيقـول سـامعه: صدقت وبررت.	truth and righteousness"[36]
ويقول عند لفظ الإقامة: أقامها الله وأدامها.	When he hears the phrase specific to the Iqāma he says "May God establish it and continue it"[37]
ويصـلي علـى النبـي ﷺ إذا فـرغ، ويقـول: ((اللهـم ربّ هذه الـدعوة التّامـة، والصـلاة القائمـة، آت محمـدًا الوسـيلة والفضــيلة، وابعثــه مقامًــا محمودًا الذي وعدته)).	He sends his peace and blessings on the Prophet ﷺ saying: "O God Lord of this perfect call and established prayer, give Muhammad the intercession and virtuous station, and resurrect him on an exalted station which you have promised him."
ثم يدعو هنا، وعند الإقامة.	Then he may make Duāʾ here and at the Iqāma.
س49: هل يحرم الخروج من المسجد بعد الأذان أم لا؟	Q49- Is it forbidden to exit the Mosque after the Adhān or not?

[36] - Al-Majd Ibn Taymiyya said "This is baseless, yet many common people frequently say it." Ibn Ḥajar held the same in al-Talkhīṣ ʾl-Ḥabīr.
[37] - Collected by Abū Dāwūd in his Sunan. One of the narrators in the chain is unknown. Despite this, Abū Dāwūd did not comment on it, indicating he held it to be acceptable. Later scholars such as al-Bayhaqi, Ibn Ḥajar, and al-Albāni indicated it is weak.

ج: يحـــرم الخـــروج مـــن المسجد بعد الأذان بلا عذر أو نية رجوع.

A49- It is forbidden to exit the Mosque after the Adhān without an excuse or the intention to return.

باب حكم الصلاة

Ruling of Prayer

س50: علـــى مَـــنْ تجـــب الصلاة؟

Q50- Who is prayer obligatory upon?

ج: تجب الصلاة على كل:

1- مسلمٍ.

2- مكلَّفٍ.

3- غير حائضٍ ونفساء.

A50- Prayer is obligatory upon:

1- A Muslim

2- Of legal capacity

3- Not in a state of menses or post partum bleeding

ولا تسقط عن الإنسـان مـا دام عقله باقيًا.

It never ceases in obligation as long as one's intellect is intact.

وتصح من مميز، والثواب له.

It is valid from a child that has reached an age of discernment, and he is rewarded for such.

ويلزم وليُّه أن يأمره بها لسبع سنين، ويضربه عليها إذا بلغ عشر سنين.	It is necessary for his guardian to order him to pray at seven and to reprimand him for not doing so at the age of ten.
ومن تركها منكرًا لوجوبها فقد كفر.	Whoever leaves off prayer, denying its obligation then he has committed apostasy.
باب مواقيت الصلاة	***Prayer Times***
س51: ما أوقات الصلاة؟	Q51- What are the times of prayer?
ج: وقت الظهر: من زوال الشمس إلى أن يصير ظل كل شيءٍ مثله سوى ظل الزوال.	A51- Ẓuhr Time: from the passing of the zenith until the shadow of an object is its own length not including the shadow thrown by the zenith.
ثم يليه الوقت المختار للعصر حتى يصير ظل كل شيء مثليه سوى ظل الزوال.	After this is the preferred time for ʿAṣr, until the shade of an object is two times its length not including the shadow thrown by the zenith.
ثم هو وقت ضرورة يحرم تأخير الصلاة إليه إلى غروب الشمس.	After this is the time of necessity, it is forbidden to delay the prayer from this time until the setting of the sun.

Maghrib time: From the setting of the sun until the redness of the sky dissipates.

ووقت المغرب: من غروب الشمس إلى أن يغيب الشفق الأحمر.

The preferred time for ʿIshāʾ is from the disappearance of the redness of the sky until the first third of the night.

ووقت العشاء المختار: من مغيب الشفق الأحمر إلى ثلث الليل الأول.

Then the time of necessity enters until the crack of dawn.

ثم هو وقت ضرورة إلى طلوع الفجر.

The morning prayer time is from the crack of dawn until the rising of the sun.

ووقت الصبح: من طلوع الفجر إلى طلوع الشمس.

Supererogatory Prayers

باب صلاة التطوع

Q52: Are supererogatory prayers recommended? Which of them are best?

س52: هل تسن صلاة التطوع؟ وما أفضلها؟

A52: Supererogatory prayers are recommended.

ج: صلاة التطوع مسنونة.

The best of them are those recommended to be performed in a group.

وأفضلها ما سُنَّ جماعة.

وآكـــدها: الكســـوف، فالاستسقاء، فالتراويح، فالوتر.

The most emphasized of these: Kusūf, then Istisqā', then Tarāwīḥ, then Witr.

وأقلُّهُ: ركعة، وأكثره إحدى عشر ركعة، وأدنى الكمال ثلاث ركعاتٍ بسلامين.

The minimum [of Witr] is one rak'a, the maximum is 11 rak'a, and the least of complete is 3 rak'a with two taslīms.

ووقتُهُ: ما بين صلاة العشاء وطلوع الفجر، يقنت فيه بعد الركوع، ولو قنت قبله جاز.

Its time is between 'Ishā' prayer time and the crack of dawn, making Qunūt therein after Rukū'; if Qunūt is made beforehand it is permissible.

والوارد فيه أن يقول:

It is narrated to say [in Qunūt]:

((اللهم اهدنا فيمن هديت، وعافنا فيمن عافيت، وتولنا فيمن توليت، وبارك لنا فيما أعطيت، وقنا شر ما قضيت إنك تقضي ولا يُقضى عليك، وإنه لا يذل من واليت، ولا يُعزُّ مَنْ عاديت، تباركت ربنا وتعاليت.

"O Allah guide us amongst those you've guided, and pardon us amongst those you've pardoned, and shelter us amongst those you've shelter, and bless us in all you've given us, protect us the evil of what you've decreed, you decree and none decrees over you, indeed one who you accompany will not be debased, and one you show enmity will not have might, you are lofty and blessed,

	Our Lord.
اللهــم إنــا نعــوذ برضــاك مــن ســخطك، وبعفــوك مــن عقوبتــك، وبــك منــك، لا نحصي ثناء عليـك أنـت كمـا أثنيت على نفسك.	O Allah we seek refuge in your pleasure from your anger, and in your safety from your punishment, and in you from you, we cannot enumerate your praises, you are as you have exalted yourself. [38]
وصلى الله على محمـد النبـي الأمي وعلى آله وصحبه)).	And grace and bless Muhammad the illiterate Prophet, his family and companions."
ويؤمّن المأموم.	The follower in prayer should say Amen.
ويكـون رافعًـا يديـه مـن أول الدعاء.	He should be raising his hands from the beginning of the Duʿā'.
وفي آخره يمسح بهما وجهه.	At then end he should wipe his face with his palms. [39]

38 - Narrated by al-Ḥasan ibn ʿAli in Ṣaḥīḥ Ibn Ḥibbān.

39 - It is reported that Imam Ahmed himself did this. Al-Majd Ibn Taymiyya said "This is the stronger of the two narrations." Meaning from Imam Ahmed. It is substantiated by the ḥadīth collected by Abu Dawūd that "the Prophet, when he would make Duʿā' would raise his hands and we would wipe his face with them." Despite the weakness in this ḥadīth due to Ibn Lahīʿa, Abu Dawūd did not comment on this ḥadīth.

س53: كم هي السنن الرواتب المؤكدة؟

Q53: How many emphasized Sunnah prayers are there?

ج: السنن الرواتب المؤكدة عشر ركعاتٍ:

A53: Emphasized Sunnah prayers are 10 rakʿa:

ركعتان قبل الظهر، وركعتان بعدها، وركعتان بعد المغرب، وركعتان بعد العشاء، وركعتان قبل صلاة الصبح.

Two rakʿa before Ẓuhr, and two after, and two after Maghrib, and two after ʿIshāʾ, and two before the morning prayer.

ويسنُّ قضاؤها، وقضاء الوتر إن فاتت.

It is recommended to make them up, and to make up Witr if it is missed.

س54: كم هي صلاة التَّراويح؟ وما وقتُها؟

Q54: How many rakʿa is Tarāwīḥ prayer and at what time is it prayed?

ج: صلاة التراويح عشرون ركعة، تُصلَّى ركعتين ركعتين في رمضان.

A54 - Tarāwīḥ Prayer is 20 rakʿa, prayed in twos during Ramadan.

ووقتُها ما بين صلاة العشاء

Its time is between Isha prayer and Witr.

والوتر.

والأفضل تقديم سنة العشاء عليها.

It is preferred to pray the Sunnah of ʿIshāʾ before praying [Tarāwīḥ].

باب شروط الصلاة

Conditions of Prayer

س55: شروط الصلاة كم؟ وما هي؟

Q55: What are the Conditions of prayer and how many are they?

ج: شروط الصلاة تسعة، وهي:

A55- There are nine conditions to prayer, they are:

1- الإسلام.

1. Islam

2- والعقل.

2. Sound mind

3- والتمييز.

3. Discernment

4- والطهارة مع القدرة عليها.

4. Purity (when possible)

5- ودخول الوقت.

5. The time being in

6- وستر العورة مع القدرة بشيء لا يصف البشرة.

6. Covering the ʿAwra (when possible) with something that does not

describe the skin.

7- واجتناب النجاسة التي لم يُعف عنها لبدن المصلي، وثوبه، وبقعته، مع القدرة.

7. Avoiding impurities that are not pardoned when found on the body, clothes, and location of the one praying (when possible).

8- واستقبال القبلة مع الإمكان.

8. Facing the Qibla (when able to).

9- والنية.

9. And intention

باب أركان الصّلاة

Pillars of Prayer

س56: أركان الصلاة كم؟ وما هي؟

Q56- How many pillars of prayer are there and what are they?

ج: أركان الصلاة أربعة عشر ركنًا، وهي:

A56- The pillars of the prayer are fourteen, they are:

1- القيام في الفرض على القادر منتصبًا.

1. Standing upright during the obligatory prayer, when capable.

2- وتكبيرة الإحرام.

2. Saying Takbīrat al-ihram

3- وقـــراءة الفاتحـــة، مرتبـــةً، وفيها إحدى عشرة تشديدة.

3. Reading al-Fātiha, in order, it having 11 shaddahs.

فإن ترك واحدة منهـا، أو تـرك حرفًا ولـم يـأت بمـا تـرك لـم تصح الصلاة، فإن لم يعرف إلا آية كررها بقدر الفاتحة.

If one [shadda] is left off, or a letter is left off, and is not compensated for then the prayer is invalid. If the person does not know except one verse, then he will recite that one verse like the duration of the Fatihah.

4- والركوع.

4. Rukūʿ

5- والرفع منه بقصده.

5. Rising up from Rukūʿ purposefully

6- والاعتدال قائمًا.

6. Standing up straight

7- والسجود.

7. Making Sujūd

8- والرفع منه.

8. Sitting up from Sujūd

9- والجلوس بين السجدتين.

9. Sitting between the two Sujūd

10- والطمأنينـــــــــــة – أي السـكون – فـي كـل ركـن

10. Tranquility – i.e. Stillness – in every pillar which is an action.

فعلي.

11- والتشـهد الأخيـر، وهـو ((اللهم صل على محمد)) بعد الإتيان بالتشهد الأوّل.

11. The last tashahhud, which is "O Allah grace Muhammad..." after stating the first tashahhud.

12- والجلـوس للتشـهد، وللتسليمتين.

12. Sitting for the tashahhud and the two taslīms.

13- والتسليمتان في الفـرض بـأن يقـول: ((السـلام عليـكم ورحمة الله)) مـرتين، أمـا فـي النفل والجنازة فيكفي تسـليمة واحدة.

13. Making the two taslīms in the Obligatory prayer, by saying "al-Salam ʿAlaikum wa Rahmatullah" two times, as for Nafl and Janāza then one taslīm is enough.

14- وترتيب الأركان – كمـا ذُكرت هنا.

14. And performing the pillars in order – as mentioned.

باب واجبات الصلاة

Obligations of the Prayer

س57: واجبات الصلاة كـم؟ وما هي؟

Q57- What are the obligations of the prayer?

ج: واجبـات الصـلاة ثمانيـة، وهي:

A57- Obligations of the prayer are eight, they are:

1- التكبير لغير الإحرام.

1. Making Takbīr (other than the first to enter prayer).

2- وقـول: ((سـمع الله لمـن حمده)) للإمام والمنفرد.

2. Saying "God hears who praises him" for the Imām and the person praying alone.

3- وقـول: ((ربنـا ولـك ا لحمـد)) للإمـام والمـأموم والمنفرد.

3. Saying "Our Lord, to you is all praise" for the Imām, the follower, and the person praying by himself.

4- وقـول: ((سـبحان ربـي العظيم)) مرة في الركوع.

4. Saying "Glory to my Lord the Great" once during Rukū'.

5- وقـول: ((سـبحان ربـي الأعلى)) مرة في السجود.

5. Saying "Glory to my Lord the Most High" once during Sujūd.

6- وقـول: ((رب اغفـر لـي)) مرة بين السجدتين.

6. Saying "Lord forgive me" twice between the two Sajdas.

7- والتشهد الأول.

7. The first Tashahhud

8- والجلوس له.

8. And sitting for the first tashahhud

وهـــو: ((التحيـــات لله، والصلوات الطيبات، السلام عليك أيها النبي ورحمة الله وبركاته، السلام علينا وعلى عباد الله الصالحين أشهد أن لا إله إلا الله وأشهد أن محمداً عبده ورسوله)).

Which is "Greetings to Allah, prayers and goodness. Peace be upon you O Prophet, God's mercy and blessings. Peace be upon us and upon the righteous servants of God. I testify that there is no one worthy of worship but Allah and I testify that Muhammad is his slave and Messenger."[40]

باب سنن الصلاة

Sunan of Prayer

س58: ما سنن الصلاة القولية؟

Q58- What are the vocalized Sunan of the prayer?

ج: سنن الصلاة القولية: منها:

A58- the vocalized Sunan of the prayer are:

1- دعاء الافتتاح، وهو ((سبحانك اللهم وبحمدك، وتبارك اسمك، وتعالى جدُك،

1. Opening Duʿāʾ, "Glory to you O Allah and by your praise, your name is blessed, and your countenance is lofty, and

---

[40] - Narrated by al-Bukhari and Muslim from Ibn Masʿūd.

ولا إله غيرُكَ)).	there is no one worthy of worship but you"[41]
2- والتّعوّذ.	2. Saying the "Taʿawwudh"[42]
3- والبسملة.	3. Saying the Basmalah
4- وقول ((آمين)) بعد الفاتحة.	4. Saying Āmīn after the Fātiha
5- وقراءة سورة بعدها.	5. Reading a Surah after it
6- والجهر بالقراءة للإمام في موضعه.	6. Reciting audibly by the Imām at the appropriate time.
ويكره الجهر للمأموم، ويخير المنفرد.	Audible recitation is disliked for one following, and it is optional for the one praying by himself.
7- وقول الإمام والمنفرد بعد التحميد: ((ملء السماوات،	7. The Imām and one praying by himself after the Taḥmīd "Filling the heavens, filling the earth, and filling what

[41] - Narrated in the four Sunan from Abu Saʿīd al-Khudri.

[42] - I.e. saying "'Aʿūdhu billāhi min al-Shayṭān al-Rajīm", I seek refuge in God from the accursed Satan.

you will from anything else."[43]

ومِلءَ الأرض، ومِلءَ ما شئت من شيءٍ بعد)).

8. Anything pronounced more than once from the Tasbīḥ of Sujūd and Rukū', as well as "Lord forgive me"

8- وما زاد على المرة في تسبيح الركوع والسجود، وقول: ((رب اغفر لي)).

9. Sending peace on his family ﷺ in the last Tashahhud.

9- والصلاة على آله ﷺ في التشهد الأخير.

10. Sending blessings on them as well.

10- والبركة عليهم فيه.

11. And making Du'ā' after the last tashahhud.

11- والدُّعاء بعد التشهد الأخير.

Q59- What are the actionable Sunan of the Prayer?

س59: ما سنن الصلاة الفعلية؟

A59- the actionable Sunan of the Prayer are many, and are called forms/appearances.

ج: سنن الصلاة الفعلية كثيرة، وتسمى الهيئات، منها:

---

[43] - Narrated in Muslim from 'Ali, Ibn 'Abbās, and Ibn Abi Awfā.

1- رفع اليدين عند تكبيرة الإحرام.	1. Raising the hands when making Takbīrat al-Ihram
2- وعند الركوع.	2. And when making Rukūʿ
3- وعند الرفع منه.	3. And when rising from it
4- ووضع اليد اليمنى على اليسرى تحت سترته حال القراءة.	4. And Placing the right hand over the left below the navel during recitation.
5- والنظر إلى موضع السجود.	5. Looking to the place of sajda.
6- وتخفيف الصلاة إن كان إمامًا.	6. Lightening the prayer if acting as Imām
7- وإطالة الركعة الأولى عن الثانية.	7. Making the 1st rakʿa longer than the 2nd
8- والتفرقة بين القدمين شبرًا حال القيام.	8. Leaving the length of a hand span between the feet while standing.

9- وقبض الركبتين باليدين حال الركوع.

9. Grasping the knees with your hands when in Rukū‘.

10- وأن يكون رأسه مساويًا لظهره.

10. Leveling the head with the back while in Rukū‘.

11- ومحافاة العضدين على الجنبين، والبطن عن الفخذين.

11. Separating the biceps from the sides, and the stomach from the thighs [in Sujūd]

12- والتفريق بين الركبتين.

12. Leaving distance between the knees.

13- ووضع اليدين حذاء المنكبين في السجود.

13. Placing the hands parallel to the shoulders when in Sujud.

14- ووضع اليدين على الفخذين، مبسوطتين مضمومتي الأصابع في الجلوس بين السجدتين، وفي التشهد.

14. Placing the hands on the thighs, open palmed with fingers together, which sitting between the two Sajdas and while making tashahhud.

15- ويقبض الخنصر والبنصر

15. One should grasp the pinky and ring finger, grasp the middle ring

من اليمين، ويحلقُ إبهامها مع الوسطى، ويشير بالسـبابة فـي التشـهد عنـد ذكـر كـل لفـظ جلالة.	with the thumb, and point the index finger during the Tashahhud when mentioning the "Majestic Phrase" [44]
إلى غير ذلك مما هـو مـذكور فـي المطولات.	There are others, mentioned in more lengthy works.

باب سجود السهو

Sajda from Forgetfulness

س60: مـا حكـم سـجود السَّهْوِ؟ وما كيفيته؟	Q60- What is the ruling on making sajda from forgetfulness and how is it made?
ج: يسنُّ سجود السّهو إذا أتى المصلي بقولٍ مشروع في غير محله سهوًا.	A60- Sajda from forgetfulness is recommended when a person praying says something legislated in the wrong place out of forgetfulness.
ويباح إذا ترك مسنونًا.	It is allowed if he left off a recommended act.

---

44 - Lafẓ ʾl-Jalāla or the Majestic phrase is used reverentially to refer to God's name.

ويجبُ:

It is obligatory:

1- إذا زاد ركوعًا أو سجودًا أو قيامًا أو قعودًا – ولو قدر جلسة الاستراحة.

1. When a Rukūʿ, Sujūd, standing, or sitting is added, even if the length of Jalsat al-Istirāḥa.

2- أو سلم قبل إتمامها.

2. Or if taslīm is made before prayer is complete.

3- أو ترك واجبًا سهوًا.

3. Or a Wājib is left off forgetfully.

4- أو شك في زيادةٍ وقتَ فعلِها.

4. Or he doubts an act was added when performing it.

وكيفيته: أن يسجد سجدتين:

Its description: to make two Sajdas.

إما بعد فراغ التشهد وقبل السّلام.

Either after finishing the last tashahhud before Salām.

وإما بعد السلام من الصلاة، لكنه يتشهد الأخير ثم يسلم.

Or after Salām from prayer, but making the last tashahhud again then Salām again.

Disliked Acts in Prayer

باب مكروهات الصلاة

Q61- What acts are disliked in prayer?

س61: مـا يكـره فـي الصـلاة للمصلّي؟

A61- It is disliked for one praying:

ج: يكره للمصلي.

1. To only read al-Fātiha in times when reading another surah afterwards is recommended.

1- اقتصاره على الفاتحة فيمـا تُسن فيه السورة بعدها.

2. To repeat al-Fātiha

2- وتكرارها.

3. To turn one's head in prayer needlessly.

3- والتفاتـه فـي الصـلاة بـلا حاجةٍ.

4. Closing one's eyes

4- وتغميض عينيه.

5. Carrying something that will busy him.[45]

5- وحمل مشغل له.

6. Laying one's forearms on the ground during sajda.

6- وافتراش ذراعيه ساجدًا.

---

[45] - Because it will distract and detract from khushū'

7- والعبثُ.	7. Frivolity[46]
8- والتخصـر أي وضـع يديـه على خاصرته:	8. Placing one's hands on his hips[47]
9- والتمطي.	9. Stretching
10- وفتح فمه.	10. Opening one's mouth
11- ووضع شيء فيه.	11. Placing something therein
12- واستقبال صورة.	12. Facing a picture
13- واستقبال وجه آدمي.	13. Facing a human face
14- ومتحدثٍ.	14. Or someone talking
15- ونائمٍ.	15. Or sleeping
16- ونار.	16. Or fire
17- وما يلهيه.	17. Or anything distracting

46 - Such as playing with one's beard, hair, hat, clothing, or similar.

47 - Due to the ḥadīth in Bukhari and Muslim from Abu Hurayra: The Prophet forbade us to pray with our hands on our hips.

18- ومسُّ الحصى.	18. Or touching pebbles
19- وتسوية التراب بلا عذرٍ.	19. Or evening out the dirt with no excuse
20- والتروح بمروحةٍ.	20. Fanning oneself with a fan
21- وفرقعة أصابعه.	21. Cracking your knuckles
22- ومسُّ لحيته.	22. Touching your beard
23- وكفُّ ثوبه.	23. And cuffing your clothes
ومتى كثر ذلك عرفًا بطلت الصلاة.	Anytime these things are done profusely the prayer is rendered invalid. [48]

باب مبطلات الصلاة

Acts that invalidate prayer

س62: ما يبطل الصَّلاة؟	Q62- What acts invalidate prayer?
ج: يُبطل الصلاة:	A62- Acts which invalidate prayer are:

[48] - The standard for knowing when one of these acts invalidates the prayer is to ask "If someone saw you doing this, and did not know you were praying, would they quickly realize you were, or would they think you are not in prayer?"

1- كلُّ ما أبطل الطهارة.	1. Everything that invalidates purity
2- و كشف العورة عمدًا.	2. Exposing the aurah intentionally
3- واستدبار القبلة مع القدرة على استقبالها.	3. Turning one's back to the Qibla while able to face it.
4- واتصال النجاسة التي لا يعفى عنها للمصلي إن لم يزلها في الحال.	4. Filth connected to the one praying in an amount with is not pardonable, if he does not remove it immediately. [49]
5- والعمل الكثير في العادة، من غير جنسها، في غير صلاة الخوف.	5. Copious actions unlike those done in prayer (not including the fear prayer) customarily deemed unacceptable. [50]
6- والاستناد قويًا لغير عذرٍ.	6. Leaning heavily on something without excuse.

---

[49] - Carrying filth is either done out of necessity, or not. If out of necessity then each situation has its own ruling. If done without necessity, like someone who carries a bloody handkerchief in his pocket, must remove it immediately else his prayer is invalid, because purity is a condition of prayer.

[50] - See footnote 47 above.

7- ورجوعه للتشهد الأول عالمًا ذاكرًا بعد شروعه في القراءة.	7. Knowingly returning to the first tashahhud after starting to recite.[51]
8- وتعمُّد زيادة ركن فعلي.	8. Intentionally adding an action which is a pillar.
9- وتعمُّد تقديم بعض الأركان على بعض.	9. Intentionally performing some pillars before others
10- وتعمُّد السلام قبل إتمامها.	10. Intentionally making Salām before prayer is finished
11- وتعمُّد إحالة المعنى في القراءة.	11. Intentionally changing the meaning when reciting
12- ووجود سترةٍ بعيدةٍ وهو عريان.	12. The presence of a far cover, while naked.[52]
13- وفسخ النيّة.	13. Annulling ones intention

---

[51] - Due to the ḥadīth in Abu Dawūd and Ibn Majah "If he stands up completely then he should not sit, and instead should make two sajda" as well as the ḥadīth of al-Mughira ibn Shuba in the Musnad of Ahmed.
[52] - Because excessive movement is needed in order to move towards this cover and cover up with it.

14- والتردُّد فيه.	14. Doubting ones intention
15- والعزم عليه.	15. Determination to do so
16- وعملُهُ مع الشكِّ في النية.	16. Acting while doubtful of one's intention
17- والدُّعاء بملاذ الدنيا.	17. Making Du'ā' for worldly pleasures.[53]
18- والإتيان بكاف الخطاب لغير الله ورسوله.	18. Using the pronoun "your" for other than Allah and his Messenger
19- والقهقهة.	19. Laughing
20- والكلام ولو سهواً.	20. Speaking, even if forgetfully.
21- وتقدم المأموم على إمامه.	21. The one following in prayer preceding his Imām.
22- وبطلان صلاة إمامه.	22. Invalidity of his Imām's prayer
23- وسلامه عمداً قبل إمامه،	23. Making Salām before his Imām intentionally, or

[53] - Like asking for a favorite dish of food or a beautiful spouse. This is disliked due to it resembling human speech.

أو سهوًا ولم يعده بعده.	forgetfully, not [immediately retracting it] to perform it after [the Imām].
24- والأكل.	24. And eating
25- والشرب سوى اليسير عرفًا لناس أو جاهل.	25. And drinking, except for what is customarily considered insignificant for a person who forgets or is ignorant.
ولا تبطل:	It is not invalid if:
1- إن بلَع ما بين أسنانه بلا مضغٍ.	1. He swallows food stuck between his teeth, without chewing it.
2- ولا تبطل إن نام نومًا يسيرًا فتكلم، أو سبق الكلام على لسانه حال قراءته.	2. It is not invalidated if he sleeps slightly then spoke, or speech was enunciated unwillingly during recitation.
3- أو غلبه سعال أو عطاس، أو تثاؤب، أو بكاء، فبان حرفان.	3. or he is overtaken by congestion, sneezing, yawning, or crying and two syllables are enunciated.

Congregational Prayer

باب صلاة الجماعة

Q63- Who is congregational prayer obligatory upon?

س63: على مَنْ تجب صلاة الجماعة؟

A63- Congregational prayer is obligatory for all five prayers upon free adult men capable of attending while resident or traveling.

ج: تجب صلاة الجماعة للصلوات الخمس على: الرجال الأحرار القادرين عليها، حضرًا وسفرًا.

Congregational obligatory prayer is not deemed valid when a discerning child is counted.

ولا تنعقد بالمميِّز في الفرْض.

Congregational prayer is recommended in the Masjid

وتسنُّ الجماعة في المسجد.

And for women, when not in the presence of men.

وتسنُّ للنساء منفردات عن الرجال.

Q64- What does the Imām bear responsibility for on behalf of the one following him?

س64: ما يتحمّل الإمام عن المأموم؟

Q65- The Imām, on behalf of those following, bears responsibility for the

ج: يتحمّل الإمام عن المأموم

ثمانية أشياء:	following eight things :
1- القراءة.	1. Recitation
2- وسجود السهو.	2. Sajda from forgetfulness
3- وسجود التلاوة.	3. Sajda of recitation
4- والسترة قدَّامَهُ، لأن سترة الإمام سترة لمن خلفه.	4. Keeping a sutra in front of him, because the sutra of the Imām is sutrah for those behind him
5- ودعاء القنوت.	5. Duʿāʾ al-Qunūt
6- والتشهد الأول إذا سبق المأموم بركعةٍ في رباعية.	6. The first tashahhud, if the one following precedes the Imām with one rakʿa in a four rakʿa prayer.
7- وقول: ((سمع الله لمن حمده)).	7. Saying "God hears he who praises him."
8- وقول: ((ملء السماء، وملء الأرض، وملء ما شئت من شيء بعد)).	8. And saying "Filling the heavens, filling the earth, and filling what you will from anything else."

س65: مَنْ الأولى بالإمامة؟	Q65- Who has more right to lead the prayer?
ج: الأولى بها:	A65- The one with more right to lead is the person with:
1- الأجود قراءة.	1. The best recitation
ويقدم قارئ لا يعلم فقه صلاته على فقيهٍ أمي.	A Cantor who does not know the legal particulars of the prayer is given precedence over a scholar who is untrained [in recitation]. [54]
2- ثم الأسنُّ.	2. Then the older
3- ثم الأشرف.	3. Then the more noble
4- ثم الأتقى والأورع.	4. Then the more pious and righteous
5- ثم يُقرع.	5. Then straws are drawn

[54] - This does not mean he is ignorant of prayer, but that he has not delved into the intricate details of prayer and its rulings. It would be expected of every Muslim, cantor or not, to know the basic rulings of Prayer such as those contained herein.

وصاحب البيت، وإمام المسجد – ولو عبدًا – أحقُّ بالإمامة.	A home owner and the Imām of a Masjid – even if a slave – has more right to lead.
والحرُّ أولى من العبد.	A free man is more rightful than a slave. [55]
والحاضر والبصير والمتوضئ أولى من ضدهم.	As person in residence, a person with eyesight, or with Wudū᾽ is more rightful than the opposite.
وتكره إمامة غير الأولى بلا إذنه.	It is disliked to lead in the presence of one more rightful except by his permission. [56]
ولا تصحُّ إمامة الفاسق مطلقًا إلا في جمعة وعيدٍ تعذرًا خلف غيره.	Prayer lead by a sinful person is invalid in all situations except in Jumuʿa and ʿEīd when other than him is not available.
ولا تصحُّ إمامة العاجز عن	The prayer of one unable to fulfill a condition or pillar of prayer is invalid except

---

55 - Due to the slave being in the service of his owner.

56 - Such as at a person's home, or in the masjid where he is resident Imam, or where he is more qualified to lead the prayer due to knowledge and piety.

شرط أو ركنٍ إلا بمثله.	behind someone of the same condition.[57]
ولا تصح إمامة المرأة للرجال، ولا إمامة المميّز للبالغ في الفرض، وتصحّ إمامته في النّفل، وفي الفرض بصبيٍّ مثله.	A woman leading a man, and a discerning child leading an adult in an obligatory prayer is invalid. In supererogatory prayers, a discerning child leading is valid, as is his leading those like him in obligatory prayer.
ولا يصحّ الفرض خلف النفل، ويصحّ العكس.	Praying an obligatory prayer behind one praying supererogatory prayer is not valid, but the opposite is.
وتصحّ المقضيّة خلف الحاضرة. وعكسُهُ حيث استويا في الاسم، فلا يصحّ عصر خلف ظهر ولا عكسه.	It is valid to make up a prayer behind one praying the present prayer, and the opposite if they are of the same name. So praying ʿAṣr is not valid behind someone praying Ẓuhr, not the opposite.
س66: أين موقف الإمام من المأموم؟	Q66- Where does the Imām stand in relation to the one following?

[57] - For example, if a person cannot pronounce the letter Ḍād or Ra, they should not lead those who can pronounce them.

ج: يصحُّ وقوف الإمام وسط المأمومين، والسُّنَّة وقوفه مقدَّمًا عليهم.	A66- It is valid for the Imām to stand in the middle of those following him, and the Sunnah is for him to stand in front of them.
ويقفُ الرجل الواحد عن يمينه محاذيًا له، ولا تصحُّ عن يساره مع خلوِّ يمينه.	A single man should stand to the right of the Imām, parallel to him. To stand on the left without one on the right is invalid. [58]
وتقف المرأة خلفه.	A woman stands behind him.
ولا يصح أن يقف الرجل منفردًا خلف الصفِّ.	It is invalid for a man to stand alone behind the row.
س67: من يُعذَر بترك الجُمُعَة والجماعة؟	Q67- Who is excused from attending Jumuʿa and congregational prayer?
ج: يُعْذَرُ بترك الجمعة والجماعة:	A67- Those excused from attending Jumuʿa and congregational prayer are
1- المريض.	1. An ill person

[58] - Due to the ḥadīth of Ibn Abbas narrated by Muslim.

2- والخائف حدوث المرض.	2. A person fearing illness
3- والمدافع أحد الأخبثين البول والغائط.	3. One who needs to urinate or defecate.
4- ومن له ضائع يرجوه.	4. One who has lost an animal and hopes for it's return
5- أو يخاف ضياع ماله، أو فواته، أو يخاف ضررًا فيه.	5. Or fears loss of wealth, loss of opportunity, and some harm coming to it.[59]
6- أو يخاف على مالٍ استُؤجر فحفظه كنظارة بستان.	6. Or he fears for wealth he has leased and must protect, such as watching over a homestead.
7- أو أذى بمطر ووحلٍ، أو ثلج وجليدٍ، وريحٍ باردة بليلة مظلمة.	7. Or fears harm from rain, mud, snow, sleet, or cold winds on a dark night.

[59] - Because loss of wealth and/or incurred harm is greater than one's clothes getting wet, which is an excuse for missing congregational prayer by consensus.

باب الجمع بين الصلاتين

Joining between two prayers

س68: هل يجوز الجمع بين الصلاتين أم لا؟

Q68- Is it permissible to join between two prayers or not?

ج: يباح الجمعُ لمسافرٍ والقصر بين الظهر والعصر، وبين العشاءين بوقت أحدهما.

A68- Joining prayers and shortening them is permissible for a person traveling, between Ẓuhr and ʿAsr, and between the two ʿIshās[60], in the time of one of them.

ويباح لمقيم مريض يلحقه بتركه مشقّة.

It is permitted for a resident who is ill and fears that if he doesn't will be overburdened.

ولمرضع لمشقة كثرة النجاسة.

For a breastfeeding woman due to the burden of profuse impurity.

ولعاجز عن الطهارة لكل صلاةٍ.

And for a person who is unable to purify himself for every prayer.

ويختصُّ بجواز جمع

Specific to [the dispensation to] join between Maghrib

60 - I.e. Maghrib and Isha'.

العشاءين – ولو صلى ببيته – ثلجٌ، وجليدٌ، ووحلٌ، وريحٌ شديدةٌ باردة، ومطرٌ يبلُّ الثياب وتوجد معه مشقة.

and ʿIshāʾ - even if prayed at home- is [the presence of] snow, sleet, mud, cold strong winds, and rain which are strong enough to dampen the clothes and cause difficulty.

والأفضلُ: فعل الأوفق من تقديم الجمع وتأخيره.

What is preferred: is to do that which is more becoming: either joining [the prayers together] early or at a later time.

باب صلاة الجمعة

Jumuʿa Prayer

س69: على مَنْ تجب صلاة الجُمُعَة؟

Q69- Who is obliged to pray Jumuʿa?

ج: تجب صلاة الجمعة على كل ذكر مكلف، ولا عذر له، وعلى مسافر لا يباح له القصر وتجب على مقيم خارج البلد إذا كان بينه وبين محل قيامها

A69- Jumuʿa prayer is obligatory upon every legally responsible male, free from excuse, and upon every traveler who is not permitted to shorten his prayers.[61] It is obligatory for a resident located outside of his city if between him and the place in which it is

[61] - Such as a person who traveled for sin, or a person who has traveled less than the minimum distance that would permit him to shorten.

وفعلها فرسخ، فأقلُّ من فرسخ.

established and performed is one *Farsakh*[62], or less than one *Farsakh.*

وهي ركعتان.

[Jumuʿa Prayer] is two rakʿa.

س70: ما شروط صحة صلاة الجُمُعَة؟

Q70- What conditions must be fulfilled for Jumuʿa to be valid?

ج: شروط صحة صلاة الجمعة أربعة، وهي:

A70- There are four conditions for Jumuʿa to be valid:

1- الوقتُ: أي من وقت صلاة الضحى إلى آخر وقت الظهر.

1. Time: That is from the time of Ḍuḥā prayer until the end of Ẓuhr prayer time.

2- وأن تكون بقرية يستوطنها أربعون رجلاً.

2. [Place:] that is be performed in a village in which at least forty men reside.

3- وحضور أربعين رجلاً ممن تجب عليهم – ولو بالإمام.

3. [Attendance:] that forty men whom are obliged to attend Jumuʿa attend, even if including the Imām.

---

62 - a Farsakh is a medieval measurement of distance. From the Persian *Parasang*, it is around 11.12 km or 6.9 miles according to the Madhhab.

4- وتقدم خطبتين.

4. [performance:] it is preceded by two Khutbas.

س71: ما شروط الخطبتين؟

Q71- What are the conditions of the two Khutbas?

ج: شروط الخطبتين خمسة، وهي:

A71- For the two Khutbas there are five conditions:

1- الوقت.

1. Time

2- والنية.

2. Intention

3- ووقوعها حضراً.

3. That they are performed in residence.

4- وحضور أربعين رجلاً ممن تجب عليهم.

4. Their attendance by forty men upon whom Jumuʿa is obligatory.

5- وأن يكون الخطيب ممن تصحُّ إمامته فيها.

5. That it is valid for the Orator (Khaṭīb) to the lead the Jumuʿa prayer.[63]

---

63 - Notice that the Khutba here is contingent on the validity of the prayer. Therefore one who is ignorant of the fiqh of prayer and is incapable to read the Quran correctly should not give the khutba.

س72: ما أركان الخطبتين؟	Q72: What are the pillars of the two Khuṭbas?
ج: أركـــان الخطبتـــين ســـتة، وهي:	A72- There are six pillars for the two Khuṭbas:
1- حمد الله تعالى.	1. The praise of God the most high
2- والصلاة على رسوله ﷺ.	2. Sending grace upon the Messenger ﷺ
3- وقراءة آيـة مـن كتـاب الله تعالى.	3. Recitation of a verse from the book of God
4- والوصية بتقوى الله – جلّ شأنه.	4. Advising of the fear of God
5- وموالاتهما مع الصلاة.	5. The two Khuṭbas preceding the prayer immediately.
6- والجهر بهما بحيث يسمع العدد المعتبر، حيث لا مانع.	6. Pronouncing the two Khuṭbas on a level in which a significant number of people can hear them without impediment.
ويحرم على سامعهما الكـلام،	Speaking is forbidden for the one who hears them,

ولو قرآنًا.	even if Quran.
س73: ما سنن الخطبتين؟	Q73- What are the Sunan of the two Khuṭbas?
ج: سننهما:	A73- The recommended acts for the two Khuṭbas are:
1- الطهارة.	1. Purification
2- وستر العورة.	2. Covering the ʿAwra.
3- وإزالة النجاسة.	3. Removing impurities
4- والدعاء للمسلمين.	4. Making Duʿāʾ for the Muslims
5- وأن يتولاهما واحد.	5. That they are performed by one person.
6- ورفع الصوت بهما حسب الطاقة.	6. Raising the voice as loud as one can when performing them.
7- وأن يخطب قائمًا على مرتفع، معتمدًا على سيفٍ أو عصا.	7. That they are delivered standing from an elevation, resting on a sword or staff.
8- وأن يجلس بينهما، فإن	8. That he sits between the two, if unable to sit,

أبى أن يجلس، أو خطب جالسًا سكت قليلاً.

or if he gives the Khuṭba sitting, a short bit of silence should be had between the two.

9- وقصرهما.

9. They should be short.

10- وكون الثانية أقصرُ.

10. The second being shorter than the first.

س74: هل يجوز تعدُّد الجمعة والعيد في البلد؟

Q74- Is it permissible to hold more than one Jumuʿa or ʿEīd in a metropolitan area?

ج: تحرم إقامة الجمعة والعيد في أكثر من موضع من البلد إلا لحاجة – كضيق المسجد وكبعده عن بعض أهل البلد وكخوف فتنةٍ-.

A74- It is impermissible to hold ʿEīd or Jumuʿa in more than one place in an area without need; [an example of legitimate need would be] cramped space in a Masjid, or it being distant from the people, or there is a fear of discord.

فإن تعددت لغير عذرٍ فالسابقة بالإحرام هي الصحيحة.

If there are several established without justification then the earliest to start the prayer is the valid one.[64]

---

[64] - These rulings, for the most part, apply to areas in which a sovereign Muslim authority rules.

باب صلاة العيدين

The Two ʿEīd Prayers

س75: ما حكم صلاة العيدين؟ وما شروطها؟ وما وقتها؟

Q75- What is the ruling of the two ʿEīd prayers? What are their conditions and at what times are they prayed?

ج: صلاة العيدين فرض كفاية.

A75- The two ʿEīd prayers are *Farḍ Kifāya.*

وشروطها كشروط الجمعة، من التوطن والعدد، ما عدا الخطبتين، فإنهما سنة.

Conditions for the two ʿEīd prayers are the same as Jumuʿa with regards to residence and numbers, except for the two Khuṭbas which are Sunnah.[65]

ووقتُها: من ارتفاع الشمس قدر رمحٍ إلى قبيل الزوال.

Timing of the two ʿEīd prayers: From the sun rising over the horizon the length of a spear until just before noon zenith.

وهي بلا أذانٍ ولا إقامةٍ، بل ينادى لها: ((الصلاة جامعة)) ثلاثًا.

It is performed without an Adhān or Iqāma. Instead a call should be made to it "Assemble for Prayer."

[65] - Meaning if one Khuṭba were delivered it would be valid.

س76: كيف صفة صلاة العيد؟

Q76- Describe the ʿEīd prayer.

ج: صلاة العيد ركعتان، يكبر في الأولى بعد تكبيرة الإحرام ودعاء الافتتاح، وقبل التعوذ، ستّ تكبيرات، وفي الثانية بعد القيام من السجود وقبل القراءة خمسًا، يرفع يديه مع كل تكبيرة ويقول بين كل تكبيرتين: ((الله أكبر كبيرا، والحمد لله كثيرا، وسبحان الله بكرة وأصيلا، وصلى الله على سيدنا محمد النبي الأمي وعلى آله وصحبه وسلّم تسليمًا كثيرا)).

A76- ʿEīd prayer is two rakʿa. Six takbīrs are made after the Takbīrat al-Ihram, and opening Duʿāʾ but before the Taʿawwudh. In the second rakʿa, after rising from Sajda and before recitation, 5 Takbīrs are made. When making Takbīr, he should raise his hands with each Takbīr and say between each "God is imminently great, All praise is to God in abundance, and Glory to God morning and evening, May God grace our master Muhammad the illiterate Prophet, his family and companions, with plentiful peace."

ثم يستعيذ في الأولى، ويقرأ الفاتحة جهرًا، ثم سورة {سبح اسم ربك الأعلى} وفي الثانية

Then, in the first rak'ah Taʿawwudh is made, then al-Fātiha should be recited audibly, then Sūrat al-Aʿlā and Sūrat al-Ghāshiya in the second.

سورة ((الغاشية)).

فإذا سلّم الإمام خطب خطبتين كخطبتي الجمعة في جميع الأحكام، لكن يبتدئ الخطبة الأولى بتسع تكبيرات، والثانية بسبع.

When the Imām makes Salām he then gives two Khuṭbas like the two Khuṭbas of Jumuʿa in all of its rulings, except that he begins the first Khuṭba with nine Takbīrs and the second with seven.

وإن صلى العيد كالنافلة صحّ.

If the ʿEīd is prayed as Nāfila prayer it is valid. [66]

س77: ما التكبير المطلق والمقيد وما حكمهما؟

Q77- What are unrestricted and restricted Takbīrs? What rulings are associated with them?

ج: يسن التكبير المطلق والجهر به في ليلة العيدين إلى فراغ الخطبة، وفي كل عشر

A77- It is recommended to make unrestricted Takbīr audibly on the night of the two ʿEīds[67] until the Khuṭba is over, and during all ten of the first ten days of Dhul-Ḥijja[68].

---

66 - Meaning if the Imam forgets any of the takbirat or all of them, the prayer is still valid.

67 - God says in the Quran "So that you may complete the count, and that you may pronounce God's greatness for what he has guided you to…" Ibn ʿAbbās said "It is crucial for every Muslim, when he sees the crescent moon of Shawwāl, to make Takbīr."

68 - The twelfth month of the Islamic calendar.

ذي الحجة.

والتكبير المقيد من فجر يوم عرفة إلى عصر آخر أيام التشريق بعد كل صلاة صليت بالجماعة.

Restricted Takbīr is made after every prayer in congregation from Fajr the day of ʿArafa until ʿAṣr on the last day of Tashrīq.

وصفتُهُ: ((الله أكبر، الله أكبر، لا إله إلا الله، والله أكبر، الله أكبر، ولله الحمد)).

Restricted Takbīr is as follows "God is Great God is great, there is no one worthy of worship but God, God is Great God is great and to God is all praise." [69]

س78: كيف حكم الأضحية؟

Q78- What is ʾUḍḥiya[70] and what is its ruling?

ج: الأضحية سنة مؤكدة.

A78- ʾUḍḥiya is an emphasized Sunnah.

ويجزئ في الأضحية: من المَعْزِ ما له سنة، ومن الضأن

Acceptable [animals for] ʾUḍḥiya are: Goats that are one year of age, and sheep that are at least six months.

---

69 - Narrated by Abu Yusuf in al-Āthār and Ibn Abi Shayba in his Muṣannaf from Ibn Masʿūd.

70 - Known as ʾUḍḥiya, Qurbani, and other names, it is the act of sacrificing an animal during the days of Eid in devotion to God.

ما له نصف سنة، ومن البقر والجاموس ما له سنتان، ومن الإبل ما له خمس سنين.	Cows and oxen must be two years. Camels must be five years of age.
ووقتُها من بعد أسبق صلاة العيد إلى آخر ثاني أيام التشريق.	The time for ʾUḍḥiya is from the end of the earliest ʿEīd prayer performed until the end of the second day of Tashrīq. [71]

باب أوقات النهي — *Time of Prohibition*

س79: ما هي الأوقات التي تحرم الصَّلاة فيها ولا تصحُّ؟	Q79- What are the times in which prayer is forbidden and if performed therein is invalid?
ج: الأوقات المنهيُّ عن صلاة النفل فيها ثلاثة، هي:	A79- Times in which Nafl prayer is prohibited are three:
1- من طلوع الفجر الثاني إلى ارتفاع الشمس قدر رمحٍ في رأي العين.	1. From the crack of dawn until the sun rises over the horizon the length of a spear according to the naked eye.

---

71 - Due to the prohibition of storing ʾUḍḥiya for more than three days, one cannot sacrifice during a time in which storing is impermissible. While the first ruling (concerning storage) has been abrogated, this doesn't necessitate the second ruling to be abrogated.

2- ومن صلاة العصر – ولو مجموعة مع الظهر في وقت الظهر إلى غروب الشمس.

2. From ʿAṣr prayer – even if joined with Ẓuhr at Ẓuhr time- until the setting of the sun.

3- وعند قيام الشمس في وسط السماء إلى أن تزول.

3. From the zenith of the sun until it moves [from its zenith].

سوى: سنة الفجر، وركعتي الطواف، وسنة الظهر بعد العصر لمن جمع.

Except for the Sunnah of Fajr and the two Rakʿas of Tawāf, as well as the two Sunnahs of Ẓuhr performed after ʿAṣr by someone who joins prayers. [72]

وسوى: إعادة جماعة أقيمت وهو في المسجد.

And except for re-performing a congregational prayer while in the Masjid.

كتاب الجنائز

Funeral Prayers

باب أحكام الميت

Rulings on the Deceased

س80: كيف أحكام الميت؟

Q80- What rulings apply to the deceased?

[72] - Notice that tahiyyat al masjid is not included in this according to the Madhhab.

ج: يجـــب للميـــت خمســـة أشياء، وهي:

A80- The deceased is due five things:

1- غسْلُهُ.

1. Washing

2- وتكفينه.

2. Shrouding

3- والصلاة عليه.

3. Prayer over them

4- وحملُه.

4. Transportation

5- ودفنُه.

5. Burial

ويسن تكفين الرجل في ثلاث لفائف بيضٍ من قطن.

It is Sunnah to shroud a man in three white cotton shrouds.

والأنثـى فـي خمســة أثــواب كذلك.

Females are shrouded in five.

والصبي في ثوب.

The male infant in one.

والصغيرة في ثلاث.

And the female infant in three.

Prayer over the deceased

باب أحكام الصلاة على الميّت

Q81- What are the conditions for prayer over the deceased?

س81: كم شروط الصلاة على الميت؟

A81- There are eight conditions for prayer over the deceased:

ج: شروط الصلاة على الميّت ثمانية، وهي:

1. Intention
2. Responsibility
3. Facing the Qibla
4. Covering the ʿAwra
5. Removal of impurities
6. The deceased being placed in front of the one praying over him.
7. The deceased being Muslim.

1- النية.

2- والتكليف.

3- واستقبال القبلة.

4- وسترة العورة.

5- واجتناب النَّجاسة.

6- وحضور الميِّت بين يدي المصلي.

7- وإسلام المصلَّى عليه.

8- وطهارتُهُما.	8. Both the deceased and the one praying being in a state of ritual purity.
س82: كم هي أركان الصلاة على الميّت؟	Q82- How many pillars are there for praying over the deceased?
ج: أركان الصلاة على الميَّت سبعة، وهي:	A82- There are seven pillars for praying over the deceased
1- القيام في فرضها. أعني به أوَّل صلاة تصلَّى عليه.	1. Standing during the obligatory prayer over it, meaning the first prayer prayed over the deceased.
2- والتكبيرات الأربع.	2. Making four Takbīrat
3- وقراءة الفاتحة.	3. Reading al-Fātiha
4- والصلاة على النبي ﷺ.	4. Sending grace on the Prophet ﷺ
5- والدُّعاء للميت. وأقلُّه:	5. Making Du'ā' for the deceased, the minimum being "O God forgive

him and show him mercy."[73]	((اللهم اغفر له وارحمه)).
6. Making Salām.	6- والسَّلام.
7. And doing these in order.	7- والترتيب للأركان.
Q83- Describe the prayer over the deceased.	س83: كيف صفة الصَّلاة على الميّت؟
A83- Prayer over the deceased is performed as follows:	ج: صفة الصلاة على الميِّت:
1. When standing in front of the deceased, he should stand at the waistline of the female, and at the chest of the male.	1- أن يقف عند وسط أنثى، وصدر ذكر.
2. Make the first Takbīr	2- ويكبر التكبيرة الأولى.
3. Then make Taʿawwudh	3- ثم يتعوذ.
4. Then Basmalah	4- ويبسمل.

[73] - This is the beginning of a longer Duʿā narrated by Muslim from ʿAuf Ibn Mālik.

5- ويقرأ الفاتحة.

5. Then read al-Fātiha

6- ثم يكبر الثانية، ويصلِّي على النبي ﷺ بالصلاة الإبراهيمية.

6. Then he should make the second Takbīr, send grace on the Prophet ﷺ with the Abrahamic Grace.

7- ثم يكبر الثالثة، ويدعو للميت.

7. Then make the third Takbīr, and make Duʿāʾ for the deceased.

8- ثم يكبر الرابعة، ويقف قليلاً ويسلِّم.

8. Then make the forth Takbīr, stand briefly, and then make taslīm.

كتاب الصيام

FASTING

باب أحكام الصوم

Rulings on Fasting

س84: بـم يجبُ صوم رمضان؟

Q84- What makes Ramadan obligatory?

ج: يجب صوم رمضان برؤية هلاله.

A84- Fasting Ramadan becomes obligatory by sighting the crescent of Ramadan.

وتثبت رؤيته بخبر مسلم

Sighting is confirmed by the testimony of an upright responsible adult Muslim –

مكلّف عدلٍ – احتياطًا للعبادة – ولو عبدًا أو أنثى.	as a precaution – even if a slave or women. [74]
ولا يكفي في ثبوت غيره من الشهور إلا رجلان عدلان.	In establishing all other months then only two upright men will do.
س85: ما هي شروط وجوب صوم رمضان؟	Q85- What are the conditions that must be fulfilled for the fast of Ramadan to be obligatory?
ج: شروط وجوب صوم رمضان أربعة أشياء وهي:	A85- Ramadan has four conditions to be obligatory:
1- الإسلام.	1. Islam
2- والبلوغ.	2. Majority
3- والعقل.	3. Sound mind
4- والقدرة عليه.	4. Ability to fast
س86: ما هي شروط صحة صوم رمضان؟	Q86- What are the conditions for the fast of Ramadan to be valid?

[74] - Due to the ḥadīth of Ibn Umar narrated by Abu Dawūd.

A86- For the fast of Ramadan to be valid six conditions must be fulfilled:	ج: شروط صحة صوم رمضان ستة أشياء، وهي:
1. Islam	1- الإسلام.
2. Cessation of menstrual bleeding	2- وانقطاع دم الحيض.
3. Post partum bleeding	3- والنفاس.
4. Discernment	4- والتمييز.
5. Sound mind	5- والعقل.
6. And intention in the evening before every day of fasting is obligatory.	6- والنية ليلاً لصوم كل يوم واجب.
Its obligation: Abstention from all things which break the fast from the crack of dawn until the sun is fully set.	وفرضُهُ: الإمساك عن جميع المفطرات من طلوع الفجر الثاني إلى إتمام غروب الشمس.
Q87- Is anyone permitted to break their fast at any time during Ramadan?	س 87: هل يجوز الفِطْرُ في رمضان لأحد؟

ج: يجوز الفطر في رمضان لحامل ومرْضع خافتا على نفسيهما، ويجب عليهما القضاء فقط. أو خافتا على الولد لزمهما القضاء، ولزم وليُّ الولد إطعام مسكين لكل يوم مدٌّ قمح.

A87- Pregnant and breastfeeding women are permitted to break the fast during Ramadan if they fear for themselves. They are only obliged to make up these fasts. If they break the fast out of fear for their children, then they must make up the fast, and the guardian of the child must feed a poor person one Mudd of wheat for every day.[75]

ويجوز الفطر لشيخ كبير.

Elderly men are permitted to break the fast.

ويسنُّ لمريض ومسافر سفر القصر.

It is recommended for the ill and those traveling (on a trip in which they shorten their prayers)

ويلزم الشيخ الكبير إطعام مسكين لكل يوم.

The elderly are obliged to feed a poor person for every day that they do not fast.

ويقضي المريض والمسافر بدون إطعام.

The ill and traveling make up their fasts without feeding [the poor].

---

75 - One Mudd is roughly 515.54 grams.

باب مفسدات الصوم

Things which invalidate fast

س88: ما يُفسد الصوم؟

Q88 - What invalidates the fast?

ج: يفسد الصوم اثنا عشر شيئًا، وهي:

A88 - Fasting is invalidated by twelve things:

1- خروج دم الحيض.

1. Commencement of Menstrual bleeding

2- والنفاس.

2. And postpartum bleeding

3- والموت.

3. Death

4- والردة عن الإسلام والعياذ بالله تعالى.

4. Apostasy from Islam (we seek God the Most High's refuge).

5- والعزم على الفطر.

5. Intending to break the fast.

6- والتردد فيه.

6. Doubting whether to

7- والقيء عمدًا.

7. Intentionally vomiting.

8- والاحتقان من الدبر.

8. using rectal suppositories

9- وبلع النُّخامة إذا وصلت إلى الفم.

9. Swallowing phlegm when it reaches the mouth.

10- وإخراج الدم بالحجامة خاصة – في حق الحاجم والمحجوم.

10. Removing blood through cupping, for both the one performing and the one it is be performed on. [76]

11- وإنزال المني، بتكرار النظر، لا بتفكر، ولا باحتلام.

11. Ejaculation induced by constant viewing, not by thought or wet dreams.

وخروج المني أو المذي بتقبيل، أو لمسٍ، أو استمناءٍ، أو مباشرة غير الفرج.

Ejaculation or the excretion of pre-ejaculate due to kissing, touching, masturbation or foreplay [breaks the fast]. [77]

12- وكلُّ ما وصل إلى الجوف، والحلق، والدُّماغ، من مائع أو غيره، مغذيًا كان أو لا.

12. Every fluid and other substance that reaches the interior of the body, throat, and brain; whether nutrient-rich or not.

---

[76] - The madhhab views wilful extraction of blood as the same as vomiting intentionally. Traditionally, the one performing cupping did so by extracting the blood through sucking the blood out, causing him to ingest some of the blood.

[77] - Pre-ejaculate breaking the fast is particular to the madhhab.

عامدًا في الكل لا ناسيًا، ولا مكرهًا، إلا في الجماع فإنه لا يتأتى الإكراه فيه بالنسبة للمُجامع.

Intentionally in all of these, not forgetfully or through coercion. Except in the case of intercourse, whereas coercion is not applicable in the case of the one penetrating.

س89: ما الذي يجب بالفطر في رمضان عمدًا؟

Q89- If one breaks fast in Ramadan intentionally, what is due?

ج: يجب بالفطر في رمضان عمدًا القضاء.

A89- If one breaks his fast intentionally during Ramadan then it is obligatory to make up.

ولا كفارة إلا بالجماع فيه، على الواطئ والموطوء باختياره.

There is no expiation due [for willfully breaking the fast] except if [broken by] intercourse during [the daytime of Ramadan] obligatory on the penetrator and the one willfully penetrated.

والكفارة هي:

The expiation is:

1- عتق رقبة مؤمنةٍ.

1. Freeing of a believing slave.

2- فإن لم يستطع فصيام

2. If he is not able to, then he must fast for two monthس consecutively.

شهرين متتابعين.

3- فإن لم يستطع فإطعام ستين مسكينًا.

3. If he is not able to, then he must feed sixty indigents.

4- فإن لم يستطع سقطَت.

4. If he is not able to, then it [the obligation] is dropped.

كتاب الزكاة

ZAKAT

باب أحكام الزكاة

Rulings of Zakat

س90: في أي شيء تجب الزكاة؟

Q90- What is liable for Zakat?

ج: تجب الزكاة في خمسة أشياء:

A90- Five types of wealth are liable for Zakat?

الأول: بهيمة الأنعام – وهي الإبل والبقر والغنم-.

First: Livestock, namely camel, cow, and sheep/goats.

والثاني: الخارج من الأرض.

Second: Agriculture.

والثالث: العسل.

Third: Honey

والرابع: الذهب والفضة.	Fourth: Gold and Silver.
والخامس: عروض التجارة – أي البضاعة المعدَّة للبيع والشراء لأجل الربح.	Fifth: Merchandise, ie wares that are presented for sale for profit.
س91: كم هي شروط وجوب الزكاة؟	Q91- What are the conditions for Zakat to be obligatory?
ج: شروط وجوب الزكاة خمسة أشياء:	A91- There are five conditions for Zakat to be obligatory:
الأول: الإسلام.	First: Islam
الثاني: الحرية.	Second: Freedom
والثالث: ملك النصاب.	Third: Possession of Niṣāb
والرابع: الملك التام، فلا زكاة على السيد في مال الكتابة، ولا في حصة المضارب قبل القسمة.	Fourth: Complete possession. Zakat is not due on a Master's wealth held in the manumission of a slave, or in a person's investment stake in a partnership before distribution.

Fifth: The passing of [one lunar] year.

والخامس: تمام الحَوْل.

The wealth of children and the insane are liable for Zakat.

تجب في مال الصغير والمجنون.

Zakat on Livestock

باب زكاة بهيمة الأنعام

Q92- What conditions apply to Zakat on livestock?

س92: كم هي شروط الزكاة في بهيمة الأنعام؟

A92- For Zakat to be liable on three types of livestock the following conditions apply:

ج: شروط وجوب الزكاة في بهيمة الأنعام ثلاثة:

First: They should be reared for breeding, milk, and husbandry, not for work.

الأول: أن تُتَّخَذ للتربية واللَّبن والولد، لا للعمل.

Second: That they graze on the land most of the year.

والثاني: أن ترعى المباح أكثر السنة.

Third: That they reach *Niṣāb.*

والثالث: أن تبلغ نصابًا.

Q93- What is the Niṣāb of camels?

س93: كم هو نصاب الإبل؟

A93- The minimum Niṣāb of

ج: أقلُّ نصاب الإبل: خمس،

camels is five; one sheep is due on five.	وفيها شاة.
Then in every additional five is one sheep.	ثم في كل خمس شاة.
Until twenty-five, then a she-camel of one year is due.	إلى خمس وعشرين وفيها: بنت مخاضٍ، وهي ما تم لها سنة.
Until 36, then a she-camel of two years is due.	وفي ست وثلاثين بنت لبون، وهي ما تم لها سنتان.
Until 46, then a she-camel of three years is due.	وفي ست وأربعين حقّة، لها ثلاث سنين.
Until 61 camels, a she-camel of four years is due.	وفي إحدى وستين جذعة، لها أربع سنين.
Until 76, then two she-camels of two years each is due.	وفي ست وسبعين بنتا لبونٍ.
Until 130, which the number stabilizes and for every 40 camels a she-camel of two years is due, and for every 50 camels a she-camel of three years is due.	إلى مائة وثلاثين فيستقر في كل أربعين بنت لبون، وفي كل خمسين حقَّة.

س94: كم هو نصاب البقر؟	Q94- What is the Niṣāb of Cows?
ج: أقلُّ نصاب البقر ثلاثون، وفيها تبيع ذو سنة.	A94- The minimum Niṣāb of cows is thirty cows, for which a bull of one year is due.
وفي أربعين مسنة لها سنتان.	For forty cows, a heifer of two years is due.
س95: كم هو نصاب الغنم؟ وما حكم الخليطين؟	Q95- What is the Niṣāb of sheep/goats? What about mixed herds?
ج: أقلُّ نصاب الغنم أربعون، وفيها شاة معزٍ تم لها سنة، أو جذعة ضأن لها ستة أشهر.	A95- The minimum Niṣāb of Sheep/goat is forty, for which one sheep of 6 months or goat of one year is due.
وفي مائة وإحدى وعشرين شاتان، وفي مائتين وواحدة ثلاث شياه، وفي أربعمائة أربع شياه.	For one hundred and twenty sheep, two sheep are due. For two hundred and one sheep, three sheep are due, and for 400 sheep, four sheep are due.
ثم في كل مائة شاة شاة واحدة.	Then for every hundred above this one sheep is due.

When one or more herds are mixed in the Niṣāb of grazing animals for the entire year, and they share in their pens, yards, milking stations, studs, and grazing lands then Zakat is paid on them as if they were one.

وإذا اختلط اثنان فأكثر في نصاب ماشية جميع الحول، واشتركا في المبيت والمسرح والمحلب والفحل والمرعى زكّيا كالواحد.

Zakat of Grains and Fruit

باب زكاة الحبوب والثمار

Q96- What conditions apply to Zakat liable on agriculture? How much is the Niṣāb? What is obligatory in this regards?

س96: ما هي شروط وجوب زكاة الخارج من الأرض؟ وما مقدار نصابه؟ وما يجب فيه؟

A96- For Agriculture to be liable for Zakat, i.e. volume measured and storable things like wheat and barley, or fruit like dates and raisins, there are two conditions:

ج: يشترط لوجوب زكاة الخارج من الأرض، من المكيل المدّخر كالقمح والشعير، والثمر كالتمر والزبيب، شرطان:

First: That it reach Niṣāb.

الأول: أن يبلغ الخارج نصابًا.

Second: That the one who must pay it is in possession of Niṣāb when it becomes

والثاني: أن يكون المزكّى

مالكًا للنصاب وقت وجوبها.	liable.
ووقت الوجوب في الحبِّ إذا اشتدَّ، وفي الثمر إذا بدا صلاحها.	Liability commences for grains when the hull hardens and in fruit and vegetables when they are ripe.
والنِّصاب خمسة أوسق، وهي ثلاثمائة صاعٍ شرعي.	Niṣāb is Five Awsuq[78], being three hundred Ṣā'[79]
فإن سقي بلا كلفةٍ ففيه العُشْر، وإن سُقي بكلفةٍ ففيه نصف العشر.	If these crops are effortlessly irrigated then 1/10 is due, and if effort is exerted to irrigate them 1/20 is due.
ويجب في العسل العُشْرُ، وأقلّ نصابه مائة وستون رطلاً عراقيًا.	1/10 is due on honey, and the minimum Niṣāb for honey is sixty Iraqi Raṭl[80].
وفي الركاز – وهو الكنز – يجب الخُمْسُ.	For Rikāz – buried treasure – a fifth is due.

---

78 - The plural of Wasaq, one Wasaq equal to 60 Ṣā'.

79 - One Ṣā' is equivalent to 2.062 Kilograms.

80 - One Raṭl is equivalent to 386.75 grams.

## *Zakat on Gold, Silver, and Merchandise*	## باب زكاة النقدين وعروض التجارة
Q97- What is the Niṣāb of Gold and silver? How is merchandise dealt with?	س97: كم هو نصاب الذهب والفضة، وكيف حكم عروض التجارة؟
A97- Niṣāb of gold is twenty Mithqāl[81], and Niṣāb of silver is 200 dirham[82], both liable for 2.5%.	ج: نصاب الذهب عشرون مثقالاً، ونصاب الفضة مائتا درهم وفيهما ربع العُشْر.
Zakat is not due on permissible gold and silver jewelry obtained for use or lending.	ولا تجب الزكاة في حُلي الذهب والفضة المباح المعدّ للاستعمال أو الإعارة.
For Zakat to be liable on merchandise the following must apply:	ويشترط لوجوب الزكاة في عروض التجارة:
1. That the [merchandise] reach the Niṣāb of gold and silver	1- أن تبلغ نصابًا بالذهب

[81] - Equivalent to 4.25 grams. The weightage for the Dīnār and the Mithqāl are equal.
[82] - One Dirham equaling 2.975 grams.

والفضة.

2- وأن يحـول عليهـا الحـول عند صاحبها.

2. That a year passes in their owner's inventory.

وتقوَّم عند تمـام السَّنة وفيهـا ربع العُشْرِ.

They are valuated at the end of the year, and 2.5% are due on them.

باب زكاة الفطر

Zakat al-Fiṭr

س98: مـا هـي زكـاة الفطـر؟ وما حكمها؟

Q98- What is Zakat al-Fiṭr? What is it's ruling?

ج: زكاة الفطر صـدقة، تجـب للفطر من رمضان على كل:

A98- Zakat al-Fitr is a charity, obligated after ending the fast of Ramadan on every:

1- مسلم. 2- حر.

1-2- Free Muslim

3- يجـد مـا يفضـل عـن قوتـه وقوت عياله يوم العيد وليلتـه، بعدما يحتـاج إليـه مـن لوازمـه الضـرورية عـن نفسـه، وعمـن

3- Who finds a surplus of food for himself and his dependents on the day and night of ʿEīd, after accounting for the personal needs of himself and those he supports from the

يمونه من المسلمين.

Muslims.

والأفضل إخراجها يوم العيد قبل الصلاة، وتكره بعدها، ويحرُم تأخيرها عن يوم العيد، وتجوز قبله بيومين لا أكثر.

It is best to give it on the day of ʿEīd before the prayer, and it is disliked after it. It is forbidden to delay it until after ʿEīd, and it is permissible to give it two days prior, no more.

وهي صاعٌ من تمر أو قمح أو زبيب أو شعير أو أقط – وهو اللبن المجمد – فإن لم توجد هذه الأصناف أخرجها من الذي يقتات به في البلد.

It is given as a Sāʿ of dates, wheat, raisins, barley, or dried yogurt. If these types are not available then the staple food of the land is given.

ولا يجزئ دفع قيمتها.

It is not acceptable to give the price [of such things].

والصاع ستمائة وخمسة وثمانون درهمًا، وخمسة أسباع الدرهم.

A Sāʿ is 685 5/7 dirham.

باب أهل الزكاة

Zakat Recipients

س99: لمن تُدفع الزكاة؟

Q99- Who is Zakat given to?

A99- Zakat recipients are one of eight categories:	ج: أهـل الزكـاة الـذين تعطـى لهم ثمانية، وهم:
1- The Poor	1- الفقراء.
2- The indigent	2- والمساكين.
3- Those working in the collection and distribution of Zakat	3- والعـاملون عليهـا - أي: المبعوثون لأخذها من أربابها.
4- For the softening of hearts	4- والمؤلفة قلوبهم.
5- Manumission of slaves	5- والمكاتبون.
6- Those in debt	6- والغارمون.
7- Non-conscripted soldiers	7- والغزاة.
8- And wayfarers, i.e. those that are cut off from their homelands.	8- وابـن السـبيل – أي المنقطعون عن أوطانهم.

كتاب الحج

HAJJ

باب أحكام أهل الحج والعمرة

Rulings on Those who make Hajj and Umra

س100: مـا حكـم الحـجِّ والعمرة؟

Q100- What is the ruling of Hajj and Umra?

ج: الحجُّ والعمرة واجبان في العمـر مـرة، بشـروط خمسـة، وهي:

A100- Hajj and Umra are obligatory once in a lifetime and have five conditions:

الإسـلام والعقـل والبلـوغ وكمال الحرية والاستطاعة.

Islam, sound mind, adulthood, complete freedom, and capability.

ويصحان من الصغير والرَّقيـق، ولا يجزآنهمـا عـن حجـة الإسلام.

They are valid from a child and a slave, but do not suffice for the Hajj of Islam.[83]

فمن كملتُ فيه هذه الشـروط لزمه السعي فوراً، حيـث كـان

Whoever fulfills these five conditions must strive to make [Hajj or Umra]

---

[83] - Meaning if a child or slave makes Hajj, then to fulfill their obligation of Hajj they must do so again when an adult or free.

immediately, if there is safe passage.

في الطريق أمنٌ.

Capability is defined as the ability to procure sustenance and transportation in excess of what one needs constantly for themselves and their families.

والاستطاعة: هي القدرة على الزاد والراحلة، فاضلين عما يحتاجه لنفسه وعائلته على الدوام.

Pillars of Hajj and Umra

باب أركان الحجّ والعمرة

Q101- What are the pillars of Hajj.

س101: كم هي أركان الحج؟

A101- There are four pillars of Hajj:

ج: أركان الحج أربعة، وهي:

1- Ihram, i.e. the intention to enter [pilgrimage] rites.

1- الإحرام – أي نية الدخول في النُسُك.

2- Standing at ʿArafa, the time for which is from the morning of the 9th of Dhul-Ḥijja until the morning of the tenth of Dhul-Ḥijja.

2- والوقوف بعرفة، ووقتُه: من طلوع فجر التاسع من ذي الحجّة إلى طلوع فجر عاشره.

3- The Tawāf al-Ifāḍa, which starts from the middle of the night of

3- وطواف الإفاضة، وأول

وقتِهِ من نصف ليلة العيد.	ʿEīd.
4- والسعي بين الصفا والمروة.	4- Saʿī between Ṣafā and Marwa
س102: كم هي أركان العمرة؟	Q102- How many pillars of ʿUmra are there?
ج: أركان العمرة ثلاثة، وهي:	A102- ʿUmra has three pillars:
الإحرام والطواف والسعي	Ihram, Tawāf, and Saʿī.

باب واجبات الحج والعمرة — *Obligations of Hajj and ʿUmra*

س103: كم هي واجبات الحج؟	Q103- How many obligations of Hajj are there?
ج: واجبات الحج سبعة، وهي:	Q104- Obligations of Hajj are seven:
1- الإحرام من الميقات.	1- Ihram from the Miqāt.
2- والوقوف بعرفة جزءًا من	2- Standing at ʿArafa for part of the night (for the person who arrived

الليل لمن وقف نهارًا.	during the day).
3- والمبيت ليلة العيد بمزدلفة إلى نصف الليل لمن وافقها قبله.	3- Sleeping at Muzdalifa on the night of ʿEīd until the middle of the night for whoever reached there before that time.
4- والمبيت بمنى ليالي أيام التشريق.	4- Sleeping at Mina for the nights of Tashrīq.
5- ورمي الجمار مرتبًا – بأن يرمي يوم العيد جمرة العقبة التي تلي مكة، وفي اليوم الثاني وما بعده يرمي أولاً الجمرة التي تلي مسجد الخيف، ثم الوسطى، ثم العقبة، كل واحدةٍ بسبع حصيات تصيب المرمى.	5- Throwing the Jamarat in order; on the day of ʿEīd throwing stones at Jamrat al-ʿAqaba (which is closest to Makka), then on the second day throwing all of the Jamarāt starting with the one closest to Masjid al-Khayf, then the middle, then ʿAqaba. Each one with seven pebbles that hit the pillar of the Jamra.
6- والحلق أو التقصير.	6- Shaving or shortening the hair
7- وطواف الوداع.	7- The farewell Tawāf

Q104- What are the obligations of ʿUmra?

س104: كـم هـي واجبـات العمرة؟

A104- The Obligations of ʿUmra are:

ج: واجبات العمرة هي:

Ihram for [ʿUmra] from outside the Haram;

الإحرام لها من خارج الحرَم.

And Shaving or shortening the hair.

والحلقُ أو التقصير.

Forbidden Acts while in Ihram

باب محظورات الإحرام

Q105- What acts are forbidden for the Muḥrim to do?

س105: ما الذي يحـرم علـى المحرم فعلُهُ؟

A105- It is forbidden for the Muḥrim to:

ج: يحرم على المحرم:

1- Intentionally wearing clothing [sewn to fit a body part] for men. For women, it is to intentionally cover the face. Covering the head is [also not permitted] for men.

1- تعمُّد لـبس المخـيط علـى الرَّجل، وتعمُّـد تغطيـة الوجـه من الأنثى، والرأس من الرجل.

2- Intentionally smelling colognes and touching

2- وقصد شم الطيب ومسّـه،

واســتعماله فــي نحــو أكــل وشربٍ.	them, using them in food and drink.
3- وإزالــة الشــعر عــن جميــع البدن.	3- Removing hair from any part of the body.
4- وتقليم الأظفار.	4- Trimming the nails
5- وقتــل صــيد البــر، والدلالــة عليه، والإعانة على قتله.	5- Hunting land animals, pointing them out, and helping those doing so.
6- وعقد النكاح.	6- Contracting marriage.
7- والــوطء فــي الفــرج، ودواعيــه، والمباشــرة دون الفرج، والاستمناء.	7- And sexual intercourse, foreplay, touching other than the genitalia, and masturbation.
س106: مــا يجــب علــى مَــنْ فعل شيئًا من هذه المحرمات؟	Q106- What does doing one of these forbidden acts mean for the one that does them?
ج: يجــب علــى مَــنْ لــبس، أو تطيّب، أو غطى رأسه، أو أزال أكثر من شـعرتين، أو ظفـرين:	A106- A person who wears clothes, uses perfume, covers his head, removes more than two hairs or nails is obligated to sacrifice a

ذبح شاةٍ، أو صيام ثلاثة أيام، أو إطعام ستة مساكين مما يجزئ من الفطرة.

sheep/goat or fast three days, or feed six indigents like he would for Fitr.

ويجب على مَنْ أتلف صيدًا له مثل من النَّعَم ذبح مثله، أو تقديم ذلك المثل عن محل الإتلاف أو ما قاربه، ويشتري بقيمته طعامًا يجزئ من الفطرة، فيطعم كل مسكين مُدًّا من القمح، أو يصوم عن طعام كل مسكين يومًا.

Whoever kills game that has an analogous type amongst livestock, must sacrifice that type, or must present that type or similar to it and use its value to feed like he would in Fitr, giving one *Mudd* of wheat to an indigent, or he must fast a day for the amount of food he has to distribute.

وما لا مثل له يُضمن بالقيمة.

Animals that do not have analogous types are indemnified by [their] value.

والحمد لله على التمام، والصلاة والسلام على خير الأنام، وعلى آله وأصحابه الأعلام، وارزقنا بجاههم حسن الختام. آمين.

All praise is due to God upon completion, and may He grace and bless the best of creation, his family and venerated companions, and grant us by their eminence a good end.

جُمعت بقلم الفقير
موسى القدّومي

Collected and penned by the penurious, Mūsā al-Qaddūmi

غفر الله له ولوالديه

May God forgive him and his parents

آمين

Āmīn

Selected Bibliography

- Al-Āthār, Abu Yusuf
- Al-Furū', Shams 'l-Dīn Ibn Mufliḥ
- Al-Inṣāf, al-Mardāwi
- Irwā 'l-Ghalīl, Muḥammad Nāṣir 'l-Dīn al-Albāni
- Al-Jāmi' 'l-Ṣaḥīḥ of al-Bukhāri
- Jāmi' 'l-Tirmidhi
- Manār 'l-Sabīl, Ibn Ḍuwayyān
- Al-Minaḥ 'l-Shāfiyāt, Manṣūr Ibn Yūnus al-Buhūtī
- Al-Mubdi' Sharḥ 'l-Muqni', Burhān 'l-Dīn Ibn Mufliḥ
- Al-Mughni, Ibn Qudāma
- Al-Muṣannaf, Ibn Abi Shayba
- Musnad Aḥmad
- Al-Muṭli' 'Alā Alfāẓ al-Muqni', Shams 'l-Dīn al-Ba'li
- Ṣaḥīḥ Muslim
- Sharh Mukhtaṣar 'l-Rawḍa, Najm 'l-Dīn al-Ṭūfī
- Sharh Muntahā 'l-Irādāt, Manṣūr Ibn Yūnus al-Buhūtī
- Sunan Abi Dawūd
- Sunan Ibn Majah
- Sunan 'l-Nasā'ī
- Al-Talkhīs 'l-Ḥabīr, Ibn Ḥajar al-'Asqalāni

8498846R00079

Printed in Great Britain
by Amazon.co.uk, Ltd.,
Marston Gate.